As I See It

A Lay Preacher's view of
Christian belief,
written with Lay Christians
in mind.

Johan Roos

Lay Preacher in the
Uniting Presbyterian Church in Southern Africa,
Presbytery of Central Cape,
and formerly Lay Reader in the
Church of England in Southern Africa,
Harare, Zimbabwe.

To
> Joy & Ricky, Andrew & Stacey,
> Robin & Cathy, and Jonathan,

for whom this book was originally written;

> with love.

I am deeply grateful to my wife, Anne, for her love, for her constant encouragement during the time it took to write and edit this book, for making many helpful suggestions, and for her diligent and careful proofreading of the manuscript.

Copyright © Johan Roos 2010
All rights reserved

As I See It
by
Johan Roos
e-mail: j.a.roos@border.co.za

ISBN 978-0-620-47155-8

Credit

It is with pleasure that the author acknowledges John Lanoue as the source of the pictures of the Andromeda galaxy (M31) used on the cover and on page (i) of this booklet.

Acknowledgements

The author acknowledges with gratitude the writers and sources of the hymns used in this volume.

Author	Copyright owner	Page no.
Allen, F. H.	--	82
Baker, H. W.	--	137
Bakewell, J.	--	52
Bayly, A.F.	--	24
Cherry, E. G.	--	118
Clarkson, E. M.	Hope Publishing Company	67 – 68
de Santeuil J-B	--	41
Downton, H.	--	78
Fullerton, W. Y.	The Carey Kingsgate Press	131
Havergal, F. R.	--	109
Marriott, J.	--	33
Mason, J	--	6
Pollock, T. B.	--	47
Rawson, G.	--	85
Samson, R. M.	The author	99
Schütz, J. J.	--	89
Watts, I.	--	83
Wesley, C.	--	33, 84, 105
von Zinzendorf, L.	--	58

Every effort has been made to identify and contact copyright holders of hymns quoted in this book. In most cases the author has not been able to do so, and wishes to apologise to any who feel that their rights have been infringed

Unless otherwise indicated, Bible quotations are from the New International Version, Copyright © 1978 by New York International Bible Society.

Table of Contents

	Preface	v
	My personal Confession of Faith	vi
1.	God	1
2.	The Sovereignty of God	7
3.	Creation	13
4.	The Trinity	25
5.	The Lord Jesus Christ	34
6.	The Biblical View of Humankind	42
7.	The Cross, the Heart of the Gospel	48
8.	The Gospel of God's Grace	53
9.	The Holy Spirit	59
10.	The Church: its Nature and Responsibility	69
11.	Worship	79
12.	The Covenant	86
13.	Baptism	90
14.	The Lord's Supper	100
15.	"That old serpent, the devil"	110
16.	The winding-up of History	119
17.	The Bible and the Word of God	132
Literature references		138

Preface

This book is not a text-book of Theology, nor is it a comprehensive hand-book of Christian doctrine. Neither is it a guide to Christian living, although aspects of the Christian life inevitably arise as implications of doctrinal issues. It is an attempt to present the main tenets of the Christian faith in non-theological and non-philosophical language so that any lay person who has a desire to learn more about basic Christian faith and doctrine will be able to make use of it, and (hopefully) find it clearly, yet simply, written.

As a scientist, I have no quarrel with the theory of evolution – it is based upon numerous observations and discoveries and was not, as some would have us believe, "introduced as an atheistic alternative to the biblical view of creation" [1a]*. At the same time, as a Christian I have a high regard for biblical truth, and in chapters 3 and 6 I have attempted to show that there need be no conflict between scientific discovery, including the theory of evolution, and biblical truth. It is a both-and, not an either-or, situation. For a much more detailed treatment of the topics discussed in chapters 3 and 6, see the author's book *He Made the Stars Also : Science, Creation and the Bible* [1b].

As the title indicates, the book contains my own, personal views; it is thus not meant as an exposition of the Presbyterian Articles of Faith (nor, indeed, of those of any other denomination), and I am well aware that, in a few places, my approach is more akin to the views of one or other sister denomination than to those of my own Church. I trust that these particular instances would be seen to fall under "liberty of conscience" which the *Interim Manual of Law and Procedure* of the Uniting Presbyterian Church in Southern Africa recognises and upholds (*Manual*, p 93).

It is my fervent prayer that all who read this little book will find their faith deepened, their understanding increased, and their vision expanded. This is but an inadequate attempt to express the sublime truths of the Christian Faith; may the Holy Spirit nevertheless use it to bring glory to God our Saviour.

---
* Literature references are shown in brackets [ ] and are listed on pp 138 ff

My personal Confession of Faith

I believe in One God, omnipotent and omniscient, who exists from eternity to eternity, the Source of all good, the Ground of all being, and the Creator of space and time. In His wisdom, and for His own purposes, He created the universe, designing it in such a way that stars and galaxies would condense from the primordial gas; that chemical elements would form in the interiors of giant stars which, when they exploded, would scatter their atoms throughout the universe; that atoms would combine to form molecules of varying complexity, the harbingers of life; so that life in all its fullness, beauty and variety would proliferate wherever He willed it: and all this without doing violence to the intrinsic nature of anything which He had made. He is worthy of all praise and worship.

I believe that this illimitable and unfathomable Being has revealed, and continues to reveal, Himself in the form of three distinct Divine Personalities, viz. Father, Son and Holy Spirit, yet one God within whose being there is exhibited a fullness of relationship, fellowship and love.

As the Father He has shown us His love and care, and calls us from our sin, our rebellion and our apathy to share in His life and in His kingdom. He calls us, too, to establish righteousness and justice on earth, and to help all in need to the best of our ability.

As the Son, He voluntarily laid His glory aside, and entered the world as one of us via a unique conception and the common experience of birth, thus bringing near the Kingdom of God. Willingly He laid down His life at the hands of men moved by fear, jealousy and bigotry – our representatives – so that He might become our Representative and Substitute in accordance with God's pre-determined plan of salvation, that forgiveness of sins and new life might become freely available through faith (trust) in Him, and that this salvation should be proclaimed to all people everywhere in His Name.

I believe that He entered the realm of the departed that He might complete His identification with us and consummate His act of self-condescension; that He was raised again victorious over death and the powers of evil, thus setting the seal on His work of atonement; and that by faith we share in His victory. In His death we see both God's implacable hatred of sin and His deep love for sinners.

As the Holy Spirit, He prepares our hearts to receive and respond to the message of the Gospel; He incorporates us into the Church, that living fellowship of believers called out of every tribe and tongue and people and nation, and is with us in our times of greatest need and deepest darkness. He continues His work of sanctification in the believer, the building up of His Church, and the extension of' the Kingdom of God, through the words, witness and work of His people.

I believe that, in God's own way and at His own time, the Son will return as King and Judge, the dead will be raised, and God's Kingdom will be established in a form that, at present, defies description. All those who trusted Jesus in their lives will be counted worthy, solely for His sake, to share His glory and His eternal Kingdom, but those who rejected Him, He in turn will reject eternally, but with great sorrow.

Abbreviations

The following abbreviations have been used during the writing of this book

ANT	Amplified New Testament	p	page
AV	Authorised Version	pp	pages
NLT	New Living Translation	vs	verse
NWT	New World Translation	vss	verses
RSV	Revised Standard Version	f	following verse/page
op cit	in the work already quoted	ff	following verses/pages
sic	as written in the original		

Chapter 1 : GOD

I have often, on a clear night and far away from city lights, looked up at the heavens and gazed with wonder and awe at the stars shining brightly overhead, and thought to myself, "How great God must be to create such a vast universe". I have watched entranced as the clouds change colour from white to gold to deep pink with the setting sun, and I have thought to myself, "How wise and skilful God must be to design colour vision so that we might enjoy such a glorious sight". And I have looked with fascination at a silkworm spinning its cocoon, and I have thought to myself, "How caring God must be to provide such protection for the vulnerable pupa as it is transformed into the adult moth".

God's greatness and power, His wisdom and His loving care – these form the core of my understanding of the Being we call God, and they provide us with motivation for worship, adoration and praise. As we read in Romans, *"God's invisible qualities – His eternal power and divine nature – have been clearly seen, being understood from what has been made"* (Rom 1:20). But we must start at the beginning.

The Bible describes God as a being far beyond our comprehension and our ability to describe Him. The psalmist cried out, *"Great is the Lord, and most worthy of praise; His greatness no one can fathom!"* (Psalm 145:3), and the prophet Isaiah, acting as God's spokesperson, proclaimed *"As the heavens are higher than the earth, so are My ways higher than your ways and My thoughts than your thoughts"* (Is 55:9). And does not modern Science lead us to the same conclusion? Who can picture the vastness of space that is measured in billions of light years? Who can grasp the number of stars revealed by modern orbiting telescopes as the boundaries of our knowledge are pushed ever farther back both in space and in time? And who is there among us who can comprehend the enormous output of energy of that primal event called the *Big Bang*? If* God created the universe, then the nature and the majesty of His Being are, indeed, far beyond all human comprehension.

---

* I have emphasised the word "if", not to express doubt, but in order not to suggest that Science "proves" the existence of God. Although the results of modern Science strongly suggest the existence of a Creator-God, this remains in essence a matter of faith.

This leads to several important conclusions. Since the Biblical concept of God far exceeds our understanding (and even our imagination), it is difficult to believe that this concept is simply a product of the human mind. Further, if we are to know and understand anything specific about God, He will have to reveal it to us. And finally, there are likely to be many aspects of God's revealed nature that might appear paradoxical, contradictory or even unreasonable to us from our limited perspective and with our finite understanding. It would be illogical to expect otherwise.

The Bible does not give us any "proofs" of God's existence, nor does it define Him. Instead, it assumes and emphasises the existence of one, personal God, and then proceeds to describe the nature, the character and the attributes of God. From the outset, let us be quite clear that there is only one God who alone is to be worshipped and glorified: *"Hear, O Israel, the Lord our God, the Lord is one"* (Deut 6:4) and *"I am the first and I am the last, the one and only God"* (Is 44:6). The Bible teaches that He is holy (Ex 15:11; Rev 4:8), that He is Spirit (John 4:24), that He is everywhere present (Jer 23:23–24), and that He *"inhabits eternity"* (Is 57:15). These few attributes of God (and there are many more!) are enough, if we take them seriously, to give us a breathtaking picture of the essential nature of God, which enriches the picture that we obtain from nature, namely God's awesome power, wisdom, and care. Let's look at them in slightly greater detail.

Holiness speaks to us of sinless perfection, and of a hatred of sin. Thus the prophet Habakkuk (Hab 1:13) speaks of God as being *"too pure to look on evil; (He) cannot tolerate wrong"*, and Isaiah warns the people that *"your iniquities have separated you from your God; your sins have hidden His face from you…"*(Is 59:2). In the same vein, the New Testament tells us that *"God is light, and in Him there is no darkness at all"* (1 John 1:5). But the word holy (holiness) has an even richer and fuller meaning. The root idea is that of *"separation"*, so the holiness of God *"denotes His separateness from creation and His elevation above it"* in contrast to false gods and the created universe, and is *"almost synonymous with supreme deity, and emphasizes the awe-inspiring side of the Divine Character"* [2]*. In a very real sense, then, the holiness of God speaks to us about His "God-ness" – it represents the essence of His Deity. To say that God is holy is to say, among other things, that He is *transcendent* -- that is, that He is truly God, self-existent, independent of His creation, exalted over all of creation, and its Sovereign Ruler. I will touch (as I can do no more) on God's mercy and love, as the complement of His holiness, in a later chapter – the God whom the Bible describes as both *light* (1 John 1:5) and *love* (1 John 4:8).

Transcendence and immanence are complementary terms, standing at opposite poles, as it were, in the description of God's relationship to creation. We have already considered God's transcendence – that is, that He is far "above" creation and independent of it [3]. At the same time, the presence of God pervades the whole of His creation and sustains it, so that creation is dependent upon God for its continued existence, and the Bible "is the story of God's involvement with His creation, and particularly with the people in it" [4]. In Christ all things are said to *"hold together"* (Col 1:17) and He is *"sustaining all things by His powerful word"* (Heb 1:3). This activity of God in creation is referred to as His *immanence*, and implies that He is everywhere present in His creation and deeply involved with it. These two aspects of God's relationship to His creation – His transcendence and His immanence – are brought together in Acts 17:24-28, *"The God who made the world and everything in it is the Lord of heaven and earth ....(He) is not far from each one of us, for in Him we live, and move and have our being"*, and in Eph 4:6, *"one God and Father of us all, who is above all and through all and in all"*. Of considerable significance in this connection is the fact that, of all religious systems, it is only the Christian faith that brings these two concepts together and holds them in perfect balance. And both are necessary for a satisfactory and satisfying doctrine of God and creation. Leaving aside theological niceties and philosophic speculation, this doctrine describes a God "out there" who is not part of His creation and who is great enough to be worthy of our worship and adoration, yet a God "near at hand" who invites us to establish a personal relationship with Him as Father and to call upon Him in time of need.

God is spirit. These words are a direct quotation from the conversation of our Lord Jesus Christ with the Samaritan woman at the well (John 4:24), and they tell us that God is not limited in space – He does not have "size", nor does He occupy a particular "place". It is because God is spirit that His presence can fill the whole universe. In awe the Psalmist cried out, *"Where can I flee from your Spirit?"* (Ps 139:7). Indeed, to affirm that "God is spirit" (not just *"a spirit"*) implies that God has an existence that is unlike anything else in all of creation – a different kind of existence that is far superior to, and much more "real" than, all material existence. The best we can do is to think of God as "pure being" which is so very real that it was able to cause everything else to come into existence [5].

Various questions arise as a result of the concepts described in the previous paragraph. The first concerns what may be called questions of "locality": "Where is heaven?", "Where is God's throne?" and "What do we mean by 'at God's right hand'?". It is fair to say that opinion here is divided. Some theologians tend to think of these terms as indicating a "state of existence" rather than as indicative of particular locality. Others, however, link such concepts as these with places in the spiritual world that surrounds us but which is, at present, invisible to us and about which we know very little – the world inhabited by angels *. The Bible seems to imply that, on very rare occasions, humans have been given a glimpse of this invisible world (Num 22:31; 2 Kings 6:17; Is 6:1ff; Acts 7:55–56 and Rev 1:1; 4:1ff). A final answer must await greater light! (Note that, although I reject all that *Spiritism* stands for and teaches, it seems to reveal the existence of such a non-material world.)

A second question concerns the statement that human beings have been created "in the image of God" (Gen 1:26–27). Let's start by considering what this term does not mean [6]:
- It does not mean that God looks like a human being. God is spirit, and as such does not possess a body or have a shape. Any attempted image of God would, *ipso facto*, be a gross distortion of the personal reality that we call God. This is one reason that Israel was forbidden to make images.
- It does not mean that human beings are god(s) incarnate. The only incarnation of which the Bible speaks is the unique incarnation of Jesus.

The fundamental ideas conveyed by the synonymous words *"image"* and *"likeness"* in the original text is that of *similarity* and *representation*. The fact that humans are in the image of God means that they are *like* God and *represent* God. So when the Bible quotes God as saying, *"Let us make man in our image, after our likeness"* (Gen 1:26), it would simply have meant to the original readers *"Let us make man to be like us and to represent us"* [7]. So humans are, in many ways, *like* God – although that likeness has become distorted and blurred by sin, but not entirely lost – and this "likeness" to God leads to a fundamental difference between man and even the most "advanced" animals. At the same time, man *represents* God and is entrusted with stewardship over nature, but is nevertheless dependent upon Him, and exists only because of the will of God [8]. Recent suggestions by a number of authors have taken this concept further: we are made like God ("in God's image") in that we have a spiritual faculty and so we can enter into a personal relationship with God.

The final question concerns the *anthropomorphisms* that we find in Scripture – that is, those numerous occasions on which God's activities are described in human terms, especially in terms of God's having a human body, but also often alluding to human experience in general. If God is spirit, how can the Bible speak about His arm, eyes, ears, face and hands, etc? The answer seems to lie in the simple fact that, if God is going to teach us about things of which we have no direct experience, such as His various attributes and His dealings with human beings, He has to teach us in terms that we can understand – even though the language is figurative, and the reality is far greater or deeper than the description we are given [9]. We must be careful to recognise such figurative use of language which attempts to describe that which is beyond our experience, at the same time we must seek to obtain as complete a picture of God as possible from the *whole* of Scripture in order to avoid acquiring an unbalanced or inadequate view in which the human analogy is overemphasised. After all, God is the high and lofty One, whose ways and thoughts, and whose very being, are far beyond our human understanding.

Let us beware of those who come to us with an inadequate doctrine of God – a god who is so identified with his creation as to be no longer its almighty, transcendent Creator, or a God who is so exalted that He is unapproachable or unreachable by mortal man. Or a god who is simply a glorified man with a human-type body, or who is but part of a pantheon of deities. Or a god whose power is limited, whose understanding is partial, or whose holiness is so diluted that it results in a tacit acceptance of human sin and rebellion.

The eternity of God. By its very nature, the Christian faith embraces many doctrines and concepts that transcend our comprehension. This is especially so when considering the doctrine of God. We cannot imagine the vastness of space or the complexity of the human brain – how then can we expect to comprehend their omnipotent Creator? And here we have a further example: the *eternity* of God.

The Bible teaches us that God is eternal: He is the *"One who inhabits eternity"* (Is 57:15 RSV) and *"the living God, the eternal King"* (Jer 10:10), whose throne *"will last for ever and ever"* (Ps 45:6). And in the words of the seers God describes Himself as *"the first and the last"* (Is 44:6) and the *"alpha and omega, who was, and is, and is to come"* (Rev 1:8; see also 21:6). Perhaps the best way for us to think of God's eternity is to think, not in terms of an endless number of years, but to realise that He is not <u>limited</u> in any way by constraints of time, just as He is not limited by constraints of space. He is thus *"elevated above all temporal limits ... and possesses the whole of His existence in one indivisible present"* [10]; He is Himself the creator of time. This implies that God's attributes are completely constant; thus His love *"is a constant force, and not a fitful emotion."* [11]. Yet God sees events in time and acts out His will and His purposes within the confines of time [12], at least in so far as they impact upon our lives and upon the history of the world, which then becomes "His story".

This, then, is the essence of my concept of the Being of God, based on the description that the Bible gives us which, in turn, is based on God's revelation of Himself to prophet, psalmist and seer. This is the Being whom I worship, the One before whom I lift my heart in praise and worship, the sovereign Ruler over all of creation, and yet who also dwells with the humble and contrite ones; the One "in whom we live, and move, and have our being", whether we acknowledge it or not. You will realise that, quite clearly, I have left out much that could still be said. Some of that material will form part of later chapters.

1. How shall I sing that majesty
    That angels do admire?
   Let dust in dust and silence lie;
    Sing, sing ye heavenly choir.
   Thousands of thousands stand around
    Thy throne, O God most high;
   Ten thousand times ten thousand sound
    Thy praise; but who am I?

2. Enlighten with faith's light my heart,
    Inflame it with love's fire;
   Then shall I sing and bear a part
    With that celestial choir
   I shall, I fear, be dark and cold,
    With all my fire and light;
   Yet when Thou dost accept their gold,
    Lord, treasure up my mite.

3. How great a Being, Lord, is Thine
    Which doth all beings keep!
   Thy knowledge is the only line
    To plumb so vast a deep.
   Thou art a sea without a shore,
    A sun without a sphere;
   Thy time is now and evermore,
    Thy place is everywhere

John Mason

Chapter 2 : THE SOVEREIGNTY OF GOD

The term "*Sovereign Lord*" occurs frequently in modern translations of the Bible (such as the NIV), especially in the Old Testament section, although the Hebrew is more literally rendered by the words "Lord God" or "Almighty God". The same is true of some of the rare occasions in which the term *Sovereign Lord* occurs in the New Testament. But does this mean that the sovereignty of God is a non-Biblical or unscriptural concept? Far from it! The sovereignty of God is clearly portrayed in virtually every book of the Bible, even if the term itself is not often employed in the original languages!

We are able to distinguish four areas in which, according to the Bible, God's sovereignty operates. These are
- in the act of creation,
- in the natural world,
- in the history of the nations of the world, and
- in the area of human salvation.

Theologically, the sovereignty of God is a highly controversial topic, and it raises enormous philosophical problems of which I am not unaware. However, if God the Creator is truly God Almighty, then it follows that He must be fully able to control His creation, and that He must be accorded the right to deal with every part of it in accordance with His sovereign will. A lesser "god" would be no god at all!

The sovereignty of God in the act of creation. In the breathtaking vision of the heavenly worship recorded by John in Revelation 4, God is accounted worthy to receive glory and honour and power because He had created all things, and by His will they were created and have their being. The same thought is echoed in Psalm 148:5, "*Let them (all created things) praise the name of the LORD, for He commanded and they were created*", and also by the prophet Isaiah (Is 44:24), "*I am the LORD, who has made all things, who alone stretched out the heavens, who spread out the earth by myself*". In His sovereign wisdom, God willed to create a universe, and to create this specific universe, for His own purposes and for His glory. He could, doubtless, have made other kinds of universes (and perhaps He has?!), but He has decreed that we should inhabit this particular corner of this particular universe, and He has endued us with intelligence, creativity and imagination in order that we might act as stewards, responsible under God, of our small corner of creation. How we have failed!

The sovereignty of God over nature. The biblical emphasis now shifts to the earth, not because God is not in control of what happens on *alpha Centauri* or in the farthest star cluster, but because the Biblical writers wrote from an earthly perspective – their focus was on how God exercised His sovereignty and displayed the outworking of His will here on earth in nature, and in the lives of the women and men whom He created. The Biblical writers are brave enough to state quite clearly that God, in ways that we will probably never understand, is the ultimate cause of both the "good" things and the "bad" things that happen in the world. Thus Amos writes, " *'I gave you empty stomachs ... I also withheld rain from you ... I sent rain on one town, but withheld it from another; one field had rain, another had none and dried up' declares the* LORD" (Amos 4:6 – 7). And Isaiah tells us, "*I form the light and create darkness, I bring prosperity and create disaster; I, the* LORD, *do all these things*" (Is 45:7).

We note, in passing, that God was in control of the processes that contributed to the establishment of the earth as a habitable domain (Genesis chapter 1). We see the development that took place as God gave form to the earth, and how life gradually proliferated upon the earth, each step in the process being pronounced "good" by the Creator. This is discussed further in Chapter 3.

We are immediately faced with the question of natural disasters: if God is sovereign, and if (as Christians aver) He is also a God of love, how do we account for floods, earthquakes, drought, fire and famine (not to mention aircraft and motor vehicle accidents) which cause the deaths of countless numbers of people and animals year by year? Here there are a number of factors that have to be considered. The first is human sin -- greed, thoughtlessness and the wilful ignoring of God's guidelines for human well-being. Greed, as when developers, with the connivance of local authorities, site residential areas in places known to be part of a flood plain. Thoughtlessness, as when hillsides are denuded of trees to provide firewood, leading to soil erosion and fatal mudslides; and the emission of greenhouse gases into the atmosphere. And we wilfully ignore God's guidelines for wholesome human sexuality, so opening the door to the spread of sexually transmitted diseases such as syphilis and AIDS. Many more examples could be given, including driving while under the influence of alcohol.

The second factor is God's justice, frequently coupled with His love: natural disasters are often seen by God's messengers, the prophets, as His judgements upon individuals and upon nations. But very often the judgement is tempered with love in that it is designed to bring the individual/nation back to God through repentance and a turning away from their sin. Thus the quotation from the prophet Amos, above, ends with the sad refrain *"'yet you have not returned to me', declares the LORD"* (Amos 4:6,8-11); a similar example is recorded in Revelation 9, verses 20-21. But a time comes, as with notorious Sodom and Gomorrah (Gen 18:20–21 & Gen 19), when judgement has to take its course – often in the form of what might well have been a "natural disaster", such as a volcanic disturbances of the earth's crust in the case of Sodom and Gomorrah[13, 14]. But, as Kidner points out, *"… its character was a judgement, not (simply) a natural disaster"* [14]. Of how many other so-called natural disasters could this not also be true?

There is a third factor that is worth considering at this point. A number of theologians, while grappling with the problems posed by destructive natural disasters, have approached the problem from a novel direction. It is suggested that, in creating (say) the earth's atmosphere, God (in His sovereign will) gave it the freedom (as He gives us freedom) to behave in accordance with its innate nature – that is, in accordance with the laws of physics, chemistry and meteorology and geology that would govern an atmosphere (or earth's crust) like ours. This would lead to phenomena such as periods of extreme weather conditions, floods and droughts, climatic changes and ice ages in the course of the earth's history, simply due to the operation of natural laws whose source is the Creator-God Himself. God is thus still in control, but He allows His creation, including nature, to act freely as it was designed to do under the operation of scientific laws. In this way the consistency and integrity of nature are preserved.

Collins [15] has expressed this point very clearly. He writes, "Science reveals that the universe, our own planet, and life itself are engaged in an evolutionary process. The consequences of this can include the unpredictability of the weather, the slippage of a tectonic plate in the earth's crust, or the misspelling of a cancer gene in the normal process of cell division. If at the beginning of time God chose to use these forces to create a habitable earth and the human beings that inhabit it, then the inevitability of these other painful consequences was assured. Frequent miraculous interventions in nature would be as chaotic as they would be in the realm of human free will."

Very often, particular phenomena associated with such natural behaviour take place at times pre-determined by God in His wisdom in order to accomplish His divine will – the destruction of Sodom and Gomorrah has already been mentioned, and one can possibly think also of the Israelites' passage through the "Red Sea", the collapse of the walls of Jericho, and the judgement upon Korah and his co-rebels (Num 16) *.

The sovereignty of God over the nations of the earth. In one prophetic book after another we read of the way in which God raises up one nation and brings down another, often as judgement meted out because of excessive cruelty, or idolatry and spiritism, or because of corruption and oppression within or by the nation concerned. Normally, those nations that God raised up were to act as God's instruments of judgement through the normal course of political upheaval and military conquest. Thus the Babylonians were raised up to exact God's judgement upon the bloodthirsty Assyrians; subsequently the Medes and Persians under the leadership of Cyrus the Persian were used, in turn, as God's instrument of judgement against the Babylonians for their own cruelty and arrogance (Jer 50:9, 18, 29-32). The Jews, too, despite being God's chosen people, were also subject to God's displeasure and discipline through conquest by other nations, and finally through captivity, because of their own gross sinfulness. Then God used the Persian king Cyrus to restore the captives to their own country, as we read in Isaiah 45: *"This is what the LORD says to His anointed, to Cyrus, whose right hand I take hold of to subdue nations before him .... I summon you by name and bestow on you a title of honour, though you do not acknowledge me ...."* (Is 45:1, 4). So the history of the peoples of the world reflects the sovereignty of God over the nations that He brought into being, even though we cannot always understand His working.

The sovereignty of God in human salvation. If, as was suggested in a previous section, God has endowed nature with the freedom to "be itself", without capricious intervention, then how much more will God not give freedom to the creatures that He made in His own image? For surely freedom

---

* I do not wish for one moment to belittle or to denigrate the miraculous element in the Bible – our God is a God of miracle. But it does seem to me that very often God accomplishes His will by means of natural processes and events, the miraculous lying in the timing of these events. I will say a little more about this in Chapter 3.

of action is one of the hallmarks of the Godhead, and will therefore be reflected in the lives of those made in the Divine image? Indeed, part of God's sovereign will was to give us, human beings, free will! And yet, paradoxically Jesus, (Matt 22:14; John 6:44) as well as the apostle Paul (Eph 1:11), taught that human beings can come to God only if He should both *call* them and *draw* them to Himself. How this dovetails with human freedom is a difficult philosophical question, but it can be answered, even if only partially, at the level of human experience.

As I look back upon my own life and God's dealings with me from my present vantage point 50 years on, it is quite clear to me that God drew me to Himself without my realising it, and despite my unworthiness, my shortcomings, my failures and sin. All that I had to do was to respond to His love. I know, too, that I had the freedom to turn my back upon His call, had I so wished. I have subsequently spoken to many about God's love, inviting them to commit their lives to Jesus as Saviour and Lord – and they, in their turn, have been free either to accept or to reject the love that He offers them. It is only after we have accepted God's gracious invitation, and look back in wonder, that we recognise God's "hand" upon our lives preparing us for such a momentous decision.

As already mentioned, the Bible tells us that God <u>does</u> choose men and women, boys and girls *"from every tribe and language and people and nation"* (Rev 5:9) so that they might be *"a people belonging to God"* (1 Pet 2:9). This "choosing" dates from the mists of eternity, and rests solely upon the sovereign will of God and upon His unfathomable love. Difficulties arise, but as a prudent theologian remarked *"we can only express a wise interest by saying that man's free will and God's sovereignty seem like parallel lines which must meet at a point in eternity, far beyond our present range of view and that, in some manner that we cannot formulate, the Divine sovereignty must not merely be compatible with, but must even imply, the freedom of created wills"* [16]. And still the gracious invitation stands: *"<u>Whoever</u> is thirsty, let him come; and <u>whoever</u> wishes, let him take the free gift of the water of life"* (Rev 22:17).

Finally, it must be noted that belief in the over-riding sovereignty of God does not make me a fatalist. God does not call us to watch the world go by, He calls us to <u>change</u> the world. He does not call us to "go with the flow", but to swim against the stream in order to show that there is a better way. He does not call us to wring our hands in despair, but to use our hands to change society, to help the needy, to liberate those who are oppressed by poverty, ignorance and sin, and to live for His glory as we invite needy men and women everywhere to turn to Jesus. When we consider mysteries of the Faith such as the Divine will and purpose, and how it could possibly accommodate human free will, just as when we consider the nature and majesty of God, it is necessary to remind ourselves of the finitude of our minds – no matter how wonderfully they have been designed by our Creator – and of our very limited view and understanding of God's Plan.

I recall the occasion when my wife was knitting a Fair-Isle jersey for our granddaughter, and all I could see was a jumble of loose threads and uncoordinated colours. But when she turned the piece of knitting in her hand over, so that I could see the other side, a striking and intricate pattern was displayed. Now there were no loose threads to be seen, and the colours blended together to reveal a beautiful design! We, too, await the time when we shall be able to view history "from the other side", when God's wonderful and just pattern will be revealed. As the apostle Paul expressed it (Rom 11:33–36):

> *"Oh, the depth of the riches of the wisdom and knowledge of God!*
> *How unsearchable are His judgements, and His ways past tracing out!*
> *Who has known the mind of the Lord? Or who has been His counsellor?*
> *For from Him and through Him and to Him are all things.*
> *To Him be the glory for ever and ever. Amen."*

Chapter 3 : CREATION

The past 150 years have been noteworthy, *inter alia*, for the popularisation of the theory of evolution and hence the debate concerning human origins. A spin-off from this has been a tendency to discredit (in the minds of some) not only the first and second chapters of Genesis, but also the chapters of Genesis that follow, right up to the call of Abram/Abraham and the origins of the Hebrew nation. I am aware that these chapters (Genesis 1 – 11) raise a number of difficulties, both of authorship and interpretation, but I am confident that many, if not all, of these difficulties will be cleared up as fresh archaeological (and other) discoveries come to light. For example, it used to be fashionable to aver that the art of writing was not known at the time of the Biblical patriarchs; to-day we know that writing pre-dated them by a considerable length of time. Again, many supposed problems have been disposed of by a comparison of the Biblical text with other ancient near-Eastern texts [17], and I, for one, am not prepared to dismiss the early chapters of Genesis simply as "myths". The language may, at times, be figurative – a common trait of Biblical literature – but I believe that it nevertheless conveys objective truth based on historical (or, pre-historical!) fact.

God and the cosmos. If you look up into the sky on a dark, cloudless night, you can see the Milky Way, a misty brightness that forms a somewhat irregular band across the heavens. The Milky Way is the main part of our galaxy, and is made up of a great number of faint stars which, separately, are invisible to the naked eye. Where the Milky Way is brightest, millions of stars are grouped together at an average distance of about 20 - 25 000 light years from Earth. Our galaxy, like the *Andromeda* galaxy shown on the front cover, contains as many as 200 billion stars. And there are an estimated 150 billion galaxies in the universe, some of them at distances of up to 14 billion light years away! Yet, unimaginably vast as the universe is, let us not forget that its Creator is infinitely greater still, just as Leonardo da Vinci is so much greater than the *Mona Lisa*, and Michael Angelo greater than his *David*.

Cosmologists assume, from the available evidence, that the universe started with some incredible burst of energy in what is now called the "Big Bang". Although the mechanism that triggered the Big Bang is still a matter of conjecture, the event itself can be dated to about 14 billion years ago and is thought to involve what is referred to as a "quantum vacuum". Cosmologists have worked their equations back to the "Big Bang" when space as we know it today did not exist, and have found that *time* also then disappears from their equations. Now, if God is the author of the quantum vacuum and of the Big Bang and if, as I believe, He endued them with their particular properties and characteristics, then He must also be the Creator of space and time, and He stands outside of both as sovereign ruler over all of creation, the God of infinite wisdom, power and might.

All of this speaks to me of the infinite God bringing about creation through His limitless wisdom, energy and power. I believe that the cosmos exists because of the will and the wisdom of God -- that wisdom which set the universe in motion and planned each step of its development so that life could develop and flourish in at least one small corner of creation, and possibly in many others. Here I am unashamedly what one might call a *naturalist:* I believe that God frequently uses natural processes – that is, processes that can be investigated and often even reproduced by scientific means -- to bring about His will and complete His intricate designs. Thus I believe that He gave the elementary particles their particular characteristics and potential, so that the universe, and the earth when it was formed some 4 billion years ago, would develop in accordance with God's laws – we call them the "laws of science", but they reflect the way in which God wished the material of the universe to behave. The subsequent development of the universe, including the formation of a planet that would be just right to sustain life, was thus in accordance with the will of God.

Within the first few fractions of a second of the Big Bang, protons and neutrons (the building blocks of atoms) would have formed, followed by hydrogen and helium. Much later, gaseous material condensed into stars and planetary systems, and stars that exerted a mutual gravitational attraction upon each other formed clusters of stars, or galaxies, like our Milky Way.

As stars form from gaseous material they heat up. Eventually their internal temperatures become large enough for nuclear reactions to occur – the conversion of more hydrogen into helium as well as more complex reactions that lead to the formation of the other chemical elements such as carbon and oxygen, nitrogen, phosphorus and copper, calcium and magnesium, all of which are essential for life as we know it. Thus the elements were (and still are being) synthesised in the hot interiors of stars, and spread through the universe when older stars explode at the end of their "lives" as *novae* or *supernovae*. These atoms, scattered through the vastness of space, become the raw materials for a new generation of stars and planets.

As our sun, together with its system of planets, contains every known chemical element (including those needed for life), it must be at least a second-generation star. Thus it could not have formed until the universe was some 10 billion years old and the earliest stars had "manufactured" the elements needed for life in accordance with God's plan and purpose.

Earth, the right place. In order for life as we know it to develop, a very special environment is needed, and earth provides just that. It is incredibly finely tuned – that is, all of earth's properties seem to be just right! To give just a few examples: the distance of the earth from the sun is just right to provide an appropriate average temperature; the gases in the atmosphere prevent too much heat escaping from the earth's surface during the night; there is a mechanism in the atmosphere that prevents the escape of earth's water vapour into outer space; the earth's magnetic field diverts harmful cosmic rays away from the earth's surface (like a magnetic umbrella) and produces the phenomenon known as the *aurora borealis*, the northern lights. Even the existence of tectonic plates, whose movement can give rise to earthquakes and *tsunamis*, are necessary in order to maintain a suitable concentration of carbon dioxide in the atmosphere so that plants could grow through photosynthesis, thus producing food for the animals and the oxygen necessary for life.

Hydrogen, carbon, oxygen, nitrogen and phosphorus atoms are able to join together to produce molecules that are essential for the existence of life. Some of these – water for example – have unique properties that enable life to exist. It seems to me that God planned it so that these atoms would join together correctly so as to form molecules of varying complexity, the precursors of life, so that life in all its fullness and variety could proliferate wherever He willed it and wherever He provided a suitable environment, such as that of the earth.

Interpreting the biblical account of creation. The question of evolution and the Bible, often phrased as *"evolution or creation"*, has been approached from a number of different angles. Some have postulated a "gap" in time between Genesis 1:1 (*"In the beginning God created the heavens and the earth"*) and Genesis 1:2 (*"and the earth was formless and empty"*). It is then suggested that the fossil record belongs to the period of this gap, during which some cosmic catastrophe occurred ending all life on earth; the rest of Genesis 1 then describes God's *re*-creation of plant, animal and human life in a period of six 24-hour days. There is little literary or scientific evidence to support such a view, however. And why would it have been necessary to re-create the sun, moon and stars? Others, again, maintain that the original creation was accomplished by God in six 24-hour days some 6 000 – 10 000 years ago. This view immediately comes into conflict with evolutionary theory and with geological estimates of the age of the earth, and its supporters are compelled to decry the work of scientists in both of these areas. (There is very little doubt that the earth <u>is</u> about 4,5 billion years old, and not 6 000 as the "young earth creationists" insist, and Christians have to face up to this fact.)

There are those who consider the early chapters of Genesis to have a poetic or symbolic significance only, and thus not to intersect with the discoveries of Science in any way at all; and then there are those who would deny the validity of any form of divine creation, and so label the creation account in Genesis as pure folk-lore. Whilst accepting an element of poetry and symbolism in the early chapters of Genesis, and also accepting the pre-scientific character of these writings, I am nevertheless convinced that the dignity, the clarity and the logical progression of the Genesis account suggest that it has a factual basis which, although not concerned with scientific detail, should at least dovetail with scientific truth. With hindsight, Genesis 1 does seem to contain the germ of the idea of life evolving from simple forms to more complex creatures, resulting finally in human beings.

There are several key factors that need to be taken into account in any discussion on creation, evolution and the Bible. The first of these is the <u>phenomenological language</u> of the Old Testament – that is, language that describes things as they *appear* to be, rather than in terms of underlying theories or speculation. So when we read in Genesis 1:21 that God created animals "according to their kinds", it has nothing to do with arguments for or against the theory of evolution: it does not mean (as some suggest) that God fixed the different "kinds" (i.e. "species") of animals so that no evolutionary development could take place. It simply tells us what we actually observe: that dogs produce puppies, not kittens, and that God is the Author of the beautiful order and variety of animal life on the earth. Examples of phenomenological language in use to-day are the terms "sunrise" and "sunset". We need to remember that the creation narrative was written before science existed, and was meant to have meaning for all people in every age.

The second factor that we must bear in mind concerns the words used in the original for "make" and "create". The word generally translated "make" is *asah*. It is used six or seven times in Genesis 1, and has much the same meaning as the ordinary English word "make". A different word, *bara*, is translated "create". It is used only three times, and this limited usage serves to emphasise its importance in the creation narrative. It has a richness of meaning that is difficult to convey in English, and can best be thought of as indicating "the creation of a new kind of existence". It is used for the creation of the universe ("In the beginning God created, *bara*, the heavens and the earth", Gen 1 vs1), for the creation of animal existence (vs 21) and for the beginning of spiritual existence (vs 27).

In deciding how to interpret the first chapter of Genesis, we need to note that Gen 1:16ff tells us that the sun was made only on the *fourth* day of creation. Surely, then, days 1 – 3 (at least) could not be 24-hour days! It suggests to me that the "days" (*yom*) in the creation narrative cannot be solar days – with St Augustine, who wrote nearly 1 500 years before the controversy over evolution reared its head, I take the "days" of Genesis 1 and 2 to be "divine days" (epochs of creation) rather than 24-hour days. This is in keeping with subsidiary meanings of the Hebrew word *yom*. And what about the light that is mentioned in Gen 1:2? This can only have come from the sun, already in existence! This light is not the light generated by the "Big Bang" as many have suggested, since the text is no longer focusing on the heavens, but is now dealing with the earth itself. Now consider the following general scenario, which is accurate according to recent scientific thinking.

The unfolding drama of creation. Some 5 billion years ago, about two-thirds of the way out from the centre of a galaxy containing roughly 200 billion stars, a system of planets was forming around a young star – an ordinary star in an unremarkable part of the galaxy (but this is often how God works, using ordinary people to do extra-ordinary things). In this new planetary system one of the nearer planets was orbiting its star at a distance of about 170 million km. The dense gaseous atmosphere prevented the light from this star from reaching the surface of this young planet, so its molten surface remained dark for millions of years ("… without form … and darkness was over the surface of the deep", Gen 1:2) . But as this planet cooled, so its atmosphere thinned out until light from the star was able to diffuse through to the surface, but scattered and refracted so that the whole surface was faintly illuminated at the same time ("'And God said, 'let there be light'", Gen 1:3). Then, as the atmosphere thinned out further, there was less scattering of the light, so that the side of the planet facing away from the star received much less light than the other side: as the planet rotated on its axis, the dark and light regions alternated. And God called the light "day", and the darkness he called "night" (Gen 1: 5; "day" 1).

Meanwhile, as the surface of the planet cooled it solidified, and as this happened water, dissolved in the formerly molten rocks, was liberated in the form of mist and vapour, and with further cooling condensed on the surface of the planet, leaving an expanse (or 'gap') between the surface waters and clouds up above. God called this expanse "sky" (Gen 1: 8; "day" 2). But cooling of the planet also produced buckling of the solid surface, so that mountain ranges were forced up and valleys and plains developed; the water, naturally, came together in the lower parts of the surface. And God called the gathered waters "seas", and the dry ground He called "land" (Gen 1: 9 – 10). And so planet earth matured.

In some way that we cannot yet understand, living, single-celled creatures appeared in the waters of the earth as the Spirit of God brooded over them (Gen 1:2). Later on vegetation started to grow on the land at God's command ("Let the land produce vegetation", Gen 1:11). Notice that the sun, moon and stars would not yet be visible: from the point of view of an (imaginary) observer on the earth they "would not yet exist", and the vegetation would rely on the indirect sunlight that filtered through the curtain of cloud ("day" 3). Eventually the cloud cover thinned out enough for the sun, the moon and ultimately the stars to become visible (verses 14–19) ("day" 4).

The next verses (20–22) contain the second use of the word *bara*, and describe the start of all animate existence: living creatures (fish and "great monsters") in the waters, insects and birds in the air (Gen 1: 20 – 23; "day" 5). Presumably this also included amphibians and creatures like dinosaurs, but the Bible is not interested in modern systematic zoology. Finally (Gen 1: 24–27; "day" 6) we have the appearance of mammals and other land animals, which culminates in the appearance (creation, *bara*) of human beings – the beginning of spiritual existence on earth – perhaps some 200 000 years ago.

A somewhat puzzling feature of the narrative is the recurring use of the phrase *"evening and morning"*. Beasley [18] points out that in ancient times, a day started with the evening, which was the time to discuss and plan for the daylight hours (morning) to follow. So perhaps this is indicative of God communicating His will ("Let there be …"), represented by "evening", and His will actually being carried out ("and it was so") represented by "morning". An alternative view, proposed by a 13th century Hebrew scholar and Rabbi, Nahmanides, quoted by Schroeder [19], interprets this phrase by going to the roots of the original Hebrew words for *evening* and *morning*. According to Nahmanides the word for evening implies far more than simply the setting of the sun – it carries also the meaning of *chaos*. *Morning* has the opposite meaning, namely *order*. So according to him the repeated phrases "evening and morning" describe a succession of small steps from chaos (evening) to order (morning) as the chaotic earth, "formless and empty" (Gen 1: 2), was converted into the ordered world of plant, animal and human life (Gen 1: 29) that was pronounced "good" by God the Creator.

Evolution and the Bible. Although a number of writers have raised objections to the theory of evolution [20, 21], many of these objections have recently been shown to be groundless. Evolution receives considerable support from the study of genetics, and most biologists accept the theory of evolution as a unifying theory of considerable power and elegance. It has become linked with atheism, but there is no reason for this **except** for the way the theory has been attacked by Christians! I, for one, do not believe that it is a theory which necessarily supports atheism, nor that Christians need either to fear it or to attack it.

For one thing, Genesis 1 itself describes very clearly that the earth evolved and that life developed from simpler forms to more complex life forms. For another, phrases such as "Let the land produce vegetation …" (Gen 1:11), "Let the waters teem with living creatures" (Gen 1:20) and "Let the land produce living creatures" (Gen 1:24) suggest natural processes akin to those proposed by evolution. It is at least conceivable that some form of evolutionary change could have been the mechanism that God used in order to create life in all its beauty and variety. This is my own view: that evolution is the wonderful mechanism that God used to accomplish His creative will. Starting with the Big Bang followed by the formation of stars and galaxies, the production of the chemical elements in stars and the birth of new stars and planets (including the earth) and ultimately the development of the variety of life forms that now inhabit the earth, including ourselves, we can see the unfolding of God's plan. It is God's creation, and He has directed the final outcome (us!), but He has used natural processes to realize His will. So we are able to praise and worship our wonderful God for His creative wisdom and power, who "implanted" the potential for the creation of all we see around us in His master blueprint even before time began, and brought it to fruition in humankind.

The genetic language enclosed in the DNA of **all** life forms, from bacteria to humans, is identical: all use the same code and the same molecular "letters" that make up the genetic instructions, and there is very strong evidence that genetic codes in the more advanced creatures, including humans, have developed from those in simpler forms. Thus modern studies in genetics provide powerful evidence in support of the theory of evolution.

Adam and Eve. Genesis chapters 1 and 2 contain what appear to be two different accounts of the origin of human beings. Although conservative scholars have maintained that these two accounts are simply complementary views of the same great event, it was left to a Christian anthropologist, E K Victor Pearce, to suggest that these two accounts refer to completely different periods in the development of the human race. In his excellent book, "Who was Adam?" [22], Pearce makes a strong case for regarding Gen 1:26–30 as alluding to the first modern humans, the primitive hunter-gatherers of the Early Stone Age period, who made their appearance some 200 000 (or more) years ago, whereas Genesis 2 and 3 have a background much more in keeping with the settled agricultural society that followed the agricultural revolution of the New Stone Age period. He therefore suggests that Adam and Eve could conceivably have been a New Stone Age (Neolithic) couple living some 10 000 years ago and whom God chose – as later He was to choose, among others, Abram, Moses, Cyrus king of Persia, and Mary – to be the vehicles of His purpose for humankind.

When we consider Genesis chapter 2, the chapter in which Adam and Eve are first mentioned, we find the tone of the passage to be far less formal and less majestic than chapter 1. The background, as mentioned above, is more in keeping with the settled agricultural society which followed the agricultural revolution of the New Stone Age period. We note, too, that there are several features that suggest that this chapter should be interpreted figuratively. These include (i) the creation of Adam "from the dust of the earth"; (ii) the way the animals were brought to Adam in order "to see if a suitable helper" could be found for him; and (iii) the creation of Eve from Adam's "rib" (better, "side"). With regard to (i), the phrase "out of the dust" suggests a common origin for animals and human beings out of the same pre-existent material and by means of the same process as it is used of man in Genesis 2: 7 and of the animals in Genesis 2:19. It also implies that God had full and complete control over the end product of the process, *viz.*, human beings.

With regard to point (ii) above, it is inconceivable that God (or the writer) would have <u>expected</u> to find a suitable helper for Adam (man) from among the animals (Gen 2: 18 & 20). But, taken symbolically, these verses emphasise that animals are, indeed, not suitable partners for man and are, in fact under man's control and subservient to him: this is suggested and implied by the fact that Adam "named all the animals". Point (iii) explains, in figurative terms, that man is incomplete without woman, that male and female are equal in the sight of God and that they have equally important roles to fulfil within their relationship since woman "was taken out of man's <u>side</u>", and not out of his foot (to be walked over by him) or out of his head (to be ruler over him)! Indeed, it appears to be a most graphic and dramatic way of emphasising the unity and equality of male and female before God, and of their mutual dependence on one another.

A further indication of the use of symbolic language is found in the references to the two trees that are mentioned in that chapter, each of which has an idiomatic connotation in Hebrew: eating of the tree of life implies living in fellowship with God, whereas to eat of the tree of the knowledge of good and evil signifies "setting oneself up as god in rebellion against the Creator", leading to a breakdown in one's relationship with God [23]. And expulsion from the Garden underlines the "no going back" nature of Adam and Eve's act of rebellion against their Creator.

In the previous paragraphs I have pointed out that there are several indications that Genesis 2 might have been written in figurative or symbolic language. A further example of this is the fact that the name Adam simply means "man" and that Adam called his wife "woman" (Gen 2: 23). So, in one sense, Adam and Eve represent all of humankind, both men and women. But I wish to make it clear that I believe Adam and Eve, though representative of the human race, to have been historical people who probably lived in the New Stone Age in a place called the Garden of Eden till God expelled them from it.

Another indication that this chapter has an historical or factual basis is seen in the reference to the Garden of Eden itself. For one thing, it is located in the correct place on earth – where the agricultural revolution started. For another, the details fit in with what is known about the agricultural revolution at the start of the Neolithic period and the developments that followed. Note the following points [22].

- We find Adam in a garden where he practises elementary agriculture: he tills the soil and we are told that he tamed and named animals, including farm animals;

- In Genesis chapter 4 we read that Adam's son Abel kept sheep while his brother Cain farmed the land;

- We are told that Cain built a city (town?). The first known cities date from this period, some 10 000 years ago.

It is of interest to note that a number of years ago the *Smithsonian* magazine published an article that included the photograph of a LANDSAT image which "appears to have located the site of the ancient Garden of Eden as described in Genesis 2, and (is) now covered by the waters of the Persian Gulf" [24]. It is a region where gold was mined until quite recently, and where the aromatic resin referred to as bdellium (Gen 2: 12) is still found in abundance. Could this possibly be the biblical Garden of Eden?

Concluding remarks. Let us be quite clear that creation in its various stages is dependent upon the will and word of God. The world in which we live, and the universe that we observe through our optical and radio telescopes, are indeed *God's* creation, and that whatever natural processes took place, they were entirely under God's control and produced the life-forms that He had planned. God did this by means of the built-in characteristics that He gave to the atoms and molecules and, on a larger scale, to the clouds of gas in space, to stars and galaxies, so that they would all react as He had decreed. Thus we can think of God as guiding the life-producing processes through His laws of physics, chemistry, geology and biology. Christians can therefore rejoice over God's creative wisdom as shown in and by evolution and in the universe that He has created.

I have endeavoured to show that it is possible to harmonise the early chapters of Genesis with established scientific fact and with current scientific theory. I do not wish to suggest that what is written above must necessarily be the way it actually happened – it is not the only possible approach – but it does at least give the lie to the oft-repeated phrase, "Science disproves the Bible". Whatever view one holds concerning the early chapters of Genesis, it is difficult to imagine writings on creation which, on the one hand, would be as non-nationalistic, non-mythological and non-polytheistic as these chapters and which, on the other hand, would be so relevant and full of meaning to all people of all ages -- the pre-scientific, the non-scientific, and the scientifically educated alike.

What, then, is the underlying teaching of these passages that is so relevant and meaningful to people of all ages? It is simply this:

> as against atheism, they proclaim the existence of God;
>
> as against polytheism, they proclaim the existence of only one God;
>
> as against pantheism, the separateness of God from His creation;
>
> as against deism, the dependence of creation upon God;
>
> as against materialism, the spirituality of both God and human beings;
>
> as against purposelessness, that man is created in God's image, to act as His representative and steward of His creation;
>
> and against anarchy and nihilism, they proclaim the rightful place of man within the creation of God.

As a Christian, therefore, I have nothing to fear, either from the new cosmology on the one hand, or from the theory of evolution on the other. Rather, I rejoice in the way in which Science reveals to us more and more about how God has worked out His plans and purposes through all the ages and in all of creation.

1. O Lord of every shining constellation
    That wheels in splendour through the midnight sky;
  Grant us Your Spirit's true illumination
    To read the secrets of Your work on high.

2. And Lord, who made the atom's hidden forces,
    Whose laws its mighty energies fulfil;
  Teach us, to whom You give such rich resources,
    In all we use, to serve Your holy will.

3. O Life, awaking life in cell and tissue,
    From flower to bird, from beast to brain of man;
  O help us trace, from birth to final issue,
    The sure unfolding of Your ageless plan.

4. You who have stamped Your image on Your creatures,
    And, though they marred that image, loves them still;
  Uplift our eyes to Christ, that in His features
    We may discern the beauty of Your will.

5. Great Lord of nature, shaping and renewing,
    Who made us more than nature's sons to be;
  Help us to tread, with grace our souls enduing,
    The road to life and immortality.

Albert Frederick Bayly (altered)

Chapter 4 : THE TRINITY

Contrary to accusations often directed at the Church, the doctrine of the Trinity was neither copied from triads found in other religious systems such as the Egyptian triad of Osiris, Isis and Horus or the Hindu triad of Brahma, Vishnu and Shiva*; nor was it conceived by a mixed group of clerics and politicians who met in conference in Nicea in 325 A.D. The doctrine of the Trinity is primarily a revealed doctrine – but, perhaps more than any other, it was revealed to the Church <u>experientially</u>, that is, through what the original disciples <u>experienced</u>.

<u>Experiential revelation of the Trinity</u>. One of the cornerstones of Hebrew religion was the <u>one-ness</u>, or unity, of God, a doctrine that is found on virtually every page of the Hebrew Scriptures (the Old Testament) and was embodied in the "Hebrew Creed" (Deut 6:4) quoted above (page 2). There is only one, true and living God. He is a personal God, not an impersonal force. Indeed, He is "beyond personality" [26]. But when the first band of disciples met Jesus, they slowly realised that here, too, was God. Some of them would have heard the Father's voice from heaven at the time of Jesus' baptism, and three of them were on the mountain of transfiguration when again they would have heard the heavenly voice, *"This is my beloved Son"*. So those early disciples would have been faced with *two* manifestations of the one God in whom they believed and whom they worshipped. They would have learnt from Jesus about the very special relationship He had with the Being – God -- whom He called Father, and they would have realised that this was an implied claim to equality with the Father (John 5:18). Jesus told His disciples that if they really knew Him they would know His Father as well, and when, in response to this, Philip asked to be shown the Father, Jesus replied, *"He who has seen Me has seen the Father"* (John 14:7 & 9), by so doing claiming to be a <u>representation</u> (and not simply a <u>representative</u>) of God. They would have heard Him use of Himself that descriptive name that God had revealed to Moses, namely "I AM" (Ex 3:14) when He said to the Pharisees, "Before Abraham was, I AM" (John 8:58 – 59); no wonder they attempted to stone Him!

---

* The famous 19th century theologian, BB Warfield, comments, "It should be needless to say that none of these triads has the slightest resemblance to the Christian doctrine of the Trinity; beyond their 'three-ness' they have nothing in common with it" [25].

And we remember Thomas' statement (for which Jesus commended him, so it was a statement of faith and not a profanity!), "My Lord and my God" (John 20:28). In chapter 5 we will look at the effect of these experiences on their assessment of Jesus; for now, suffice it to say that they saw Jesus as another like the Father. Yet they still firmly believed that there was only one true God!

The disciples would have remembered Jesus' final injunction not to leave Jerusalem until something special had happened to them. And, indeed, ten days after the ascension of their Lord, they suddenly experienced the Holy Spirit coming upon them with divine power. They were given the ability to make themselves understood by visitors who spoke foreign languages, and they discovered a new boldness to witness to the Lordship of Christ in the face of Jewish (and, later, Roman) opposition. They would then have remembered the Lord's promise that He would send them *"another Counsellor, ... the Holy Spirit, whom the Father will send in My name"* (John 14:16 & 26).

This now made sense, because they had experienced the presence of the Spirit poured out upon them and active in the world. Here, then, was a *third* manifestation of God, namely the Holy Spirit, whom Jesus had already intimately linked with the Father and the Son in that great commission that He gave them, that they were to *"go and make disciples of all nations, baptising them in the name of the Father and of the Son and of the Holy Spirit"* (Matt 28:19) (singular ***name***, not ***names***). Some of them will have thought back to that scene at the Jordan river three short years before, when Jesus had been baptised by John the Baptist, when the Father's voice had spoken from heaven, and the Holy Spirit in the form of a dove had alighted on the head of Jesus: a glimpse, even if little understood at the time, of the tri-unity which is the essence of the Godhead. So through the experiences of those early disciples the one true God was revealing Himself as Father and Son and Holy Spirit.

New Testament evidence. This realisation soon showed itself in the writings that these early disciples left behind, i.e. the New Testament. The writers showed no hesitation in applying to Jesus Old Testament passages that spoke of God (Yahweh), yet He was not to be confused with God the Father or with the Holy Spirit; nor was there any suggestion that they thought of this as either contradictory or blasphemous. After all, they had experienced the threesome-ness of God in their lives, and this made philosophical speculation unnecessary – hence we find no formal statement of the doctrine of the Trinity in the New Testament, nor is the term "Trinity" even mentioned. But it is frequently implied, as in John 15:26, *"When the Counsellor comes, whom I will send to you from the Father, the Spirit of truth who goes out from the Father, He will testify about me"*. Here it is implied that the Spirit is distinct from the Son and yet, like Him, has His eternal home in fellowship with the Father from whom He, like the Son, comes to do His saving work sent, in this instance, not by the Father (as in John 14:20), but by the Son. Then in John 16: 14-15 we read that the Spirit comes to apply the Son's completed work of redemption, and in doing so brings glory to the Son who shares in all that belongs to the Father.

Similar Trinitarian passages are found in, for example, Heb 2:3–4; 1 Pet 4:13–14; 1 John 5:4–8; Jude 20–21 and Rev 1:4–6. Typical of such passages is 1 Pet 1:2: *"(You) have been chosen according to the foreknowledge of God the Father, through the sanctifying work of the Spirit, for obedience to Jesus Christ and sprinkling by His blood"*. In the minds of the various authors it is assumed that redemption emanates from a three-fold source, namely God the Father, Jesus Christ the Son and the Holy Spirit, "and these three Persons repeatedly come forward together in the expression of Christian hope or the aspirations of Christian devotion" [27].

We find exactly the same situation when we examine the epistles of Paul where, if anything, the interrelationship between Father, Son and Spirit is even more frequently portrayed and all are seen as co-sources of all the saving blessings which come to believers in Christ. At the same time, Paul exhibits an intense monotheism; 1 Cor 8:4, for example, expresses this when he writes, *"We know that an idol is nothing at all, ... and that there is no God but one"*, and so does 1 Tim 1:17, *"Now to the King eternal, immortal, invisible, the only God, be honour and glory for ever and ever"*. Yet he forcefully expresses the deity of the Lord Jesus Christ (again without any sense of contradiction): He is *"our great God and Saviour"* (Titus 2:13) and *"God over all"* (Rom 9:5), and Paul expressly states (Col 2:9) that *"all the fullness of the Deity lives in bodily form"* in Christ – a declaration that "the very essence of deity was present in totality in Jesus" [28]; yet He is not to be confused with God the Father. All three are brought together into focus in "the Grace" (2 Cor 13:14):*"May the grace of the Lord Jesus Christ, and the love of God and the fellowship of the Holy Spirit be with you all"* *.

---

* Careful scrutiny of many of the apostle Paul's statements reveals that, in a number of instances, he uses the term *God* [**footnote continued on next page**]

Formulation of the doctrine of the Trinity. It is as a result of this Biblical evidence – the twin strands that there is only one God, and that the Son and the Holy Spirit are equally representations of God -- that the doctrine of the Trinity was formulated by the early Church in order to define its faith more fully. It is a doctrine that could not have been discovered by human intuition, philosophical reflection or scientific observation; like so many other doctrines of the Christian faith, it had to be revealed to us by God Himself, and I have tried to show how this revelation came, initially through the first-hand experiences of the disciples, and subsequently through their writings as they were guided by that same Holy Spirit (John 14:26; 2 Tim 3:16). The formal statement of the doctrine speaks about the one God who eternally exists as three Persons, each of whom is fully God.

The use of the word "Persons" here is unfortunate, as we have a pre-conceived idea of what is meant by "person", namely an independent individual who possesses a body. But this is not quite what is meant by the word in this context; it is intended to convey the concept of *personality*, and personality that is *distinct* from that of the other two Persons and yet one in the unity of the Godhead. Although the use of the word "person" has caused misunderstandings at times, such as that we are dealing with three separate Beings, unfortunately we have nothing better.

The concept of the Trinity is unlike anything in human experience, and no illustration or analogy exists that is not without severe shortcomings. Attempts have been made to liken the Trinity to the experience of love in marriage – there is the one who loves, there is the beloved, and there is the love that exists between them within the unity of the marriage, as constituting the three "elements" in the analogy. But clearly this falls far short as an analogy of the Trinity. An illustration that appeals to me as a scientist is based on the three forms of the compound H_2O that we call water, namely ice, liquid water and water vapour. Each form is completely water, and all consist of the

---

(cont.) as an abbreviation for "God the Father", as for example in the statement of the "Grace" just quoted. This is not surprising, as "God" to the Jews described the invisible Being whose dwelling was in heaven. Then the believers came to know the Son and the Spirit whom they experienced as being active on earth, while God the Father would be thought of as remaining in heaven as "God".

same substance, H_2O. Yet they have different properties and functions, just as we believe the different members of the Trinity have different roles within the Godhead, and fulfil different functions with respect both to creation and redemption. But all illustrations fall far short of the reality!

Traces of the Trinity in the Old Testament. In order to prevent the revelation of the Trinity from degenerating into polytheism, it was necessary first to lay a firm foundation of monotheism. This was done primarily through the Law and the messages of the prophets, but in fact the whole Old Testament bears witness to the way in which God called to people to turn aside from their multitude of idols, to turn to Him, the only true God, and to worship and serve Him alone. Once this foundation had been securely laid, the revelation of God-as-Trinity could be given. At the same time, the revelation of the Trinity was largely associated with God's act of redemption in Jesus Christ, and the application thereof in the lives of men and women through the activity of the Holy Spirit. As Warfield so aptly remarks [29], "the times were not ripe for the revelation of the Trinity in the unity of the Godhead until the fullness of the time had come for God to send forth His Son unto redemption, and His Spirit unto sanctification". It was therefore not possible for the revelation to be made explicit in the pages of the Old Testament.

On the other hand, if God has existed as Tri-unity from all eternity, and if the Old Testament Scriptures are God's self-revelation and the record of God's dealings with humans, then it is to be expected that the Old Testament would contain whispers, at least, of the existence of the Trinity. And this is indeed the case. They are not sufficiently clear to lead us to the doctrine of the Trinity in and of themselves, but there are turns of phrase and scattered incidents which, if we are willing to read the Old Testament in the light of the New, give us an indication that the Deity is not a simple, isolated One. Rather, He is a God who, at the very core of His existence, embraces a complex unity that makes possible, within His own Being, a fullness of inter-personal communion, fellowship and love.

What, then, are these "turns of phrase and scattered incidents" that anticipate the New Testament revelation of the Trinity? To mention but a few: in the very first chapter of the Bible God says "let us make man in our image, in our likeness" (Gen 1:26). Some commentators take this as a "plural of majesty", but such a construction is unknown elsewhere in Old Testament Hebrew [30], though it occurs in Greek, and the context rules out the possibility that God is speaking to angels. Similar language is used in Gen 3:23 and 11:7, and Is 6:8.

Then there are a number of passages in which one person is called "God" or "the LORD" and is distinguished from another person who is also referred to as "God". Thus in Ps 45:6–7 two separate persons are called "God", and the New Testament author of the book *Hebrews* applies this passage to Christ. Similarly, Malachi 3:1-2 refers to two separate divine persons, both of whom can be called "Lord", and in Zech 2:9–11 we read that the LORD Almighty will send the LORD, who will live among His people. [Note that the word "LORD" here renders the Hebrew *Yaweh* ("Jehovah"), the special, untranslatable Hebrew covenant name for God.] In addition to instances such as those above, several Old Testament passages speak about "the angel of the LORD" and suggest a plurality of persons in the Godhead, since at times this angel of the LORD is referred to as 'God' or 'the LORD', thus suggesting that He is a manifestation of one of the divine Persons.

<u>Distinctions between Father, Son and Holy Spirit</u>. Scripture reveals to us that the Persons of the Trinity have different functions with respect both to creation and to redemption. Considering firstly the act of creation, although each is active in every part of the process of creation, the Father is the main *source* of creation (1 Cor 8:6; Eph 2:9 & Eph 3:9), the Son is the *active agent* in creation (everything was created by or *through* the Son, John 1:3 & 10, Col 1:16 and Heb 1:2 & 10), and the Holy Spirit is represented as *hovering over* creation in its earliest stages (Gen 1:3), nurturing, protecting and caring for it [**31**].

But it is in the area of redemption that we see the functions of the three Divine Persons differentiated most clearly, to reveal the wonder of the provision that God made for our salvation and to serve as a source of worship and adoration, not only for time, but also for eternity. Thus God the Father is the *source* of redemption: He planned it, and out of love sent His Son into the world as the Saviour (John 3:16). The Son willingly accepted the role of sin-bearer. He gave up His glory and the close fellowship that He shared with the Father, humbled Himself by taking human nature, and accepted the limitations implied by the incarnation (i.e., by "becoming man") (Gal 4:4). His earthly life was characterised by service rendered to others; then, finally, He gave Himself over as a sin-offering and in the process endured the divine judgement upon sin (Is 53:4–6, John 6:38–40 and Heb 10:5–10). After the Son had returned to

His Father in triumph, the Holy Spirit was sent by the Father and the Son to apply the redemption that the Son had won for us by His death, convicting men and women of sin and of judgement (John 16:8), bringing regeneration and new life (John 3: 5 – 8), transforming our characters (Gal 5:16 – 26), and equipping and empowering us for service (Acts 1:8, 1 Cor 12: 7 – 11). "In general, the work of the Holy Spirit seems to be to bring to completion the work that has been planned by God the Father and put into effect by God the Son" [32].

From what has just been written, it seems that the three persons of the Trinity, though equal in deity and of the same divine essence ("substance") as each other, are not all equal in the way they function within the unity of the Godhead. The Son and the Spirit are subordinate to the Father in the roles they fulfil both with regard to creation and with regard to redemption. The Father sends the Son, and the Son willingly responds to the will of the Father. The Holy Spirit comes under the authority of both the Father and the Son – each alike has authority to send the Holy Spirit to do the work of God in the world.

Concluding remarks and application of the doctrine. It needs to be reiterated that the doctrine of the Trinity is not a fabrication of the human mind, but a sincere attempt to summarise the various strands of Biblical evidence regarding the inter-relationship between Father, Son and Holy Spirit. There are three distinct strands that have to be taken into account [33]:
- God has revealed Himself in three distinct Persons.
- Each Person is fully God.
- There is but one God.

Although we can perhaps understand each of these statements on its own, we are unable to picture the reality that lies behind them when all three are taken together. This is not surprising, since we are dealing here with "the deep things of God". All we can do is to approach the doctrine – and Him who is the Living Reality of which the doctrine is but an inadequate reflection – with humility and with faith, acknowledging our inherent limitations.

There are a number of dangers and pitfalls that have to be avoided. The first is that we give way to rationalism, ignoring the Biblical evidence, paradoxical as it is, and reduce God to a single Divine Entity. This is then a creation of the human mind and no longer the God of creation or the God of redemption; nor is he the God of the Bible. The opposite error is to separate the Divine Persons completely, ignoring the Biblical stress on the unity of God, and so to end up with three separate gods. In practice, many of us who mentally accept the Biblical doctrine of the Trinity are prone to doing this in our attempts to "make sense" of the being of God in our own thinking. We have to guard against this tendency, remembering that there is but one God. A third error, superficially very attractive, is to think of the Persons in the Trinity simply as three possible "manifestations" of the one God, and which show themselves at different times – now God appears as the Father, now He shows Himself as the Son, and at other times He might reveal Himself as the Holy Spirit. But this view, clearly, does not do justice to the individuality of the separate Persons within the Godhead.

In his delightful little book, *Your God is Too Small* [34], Dr JB Phillips explores various inadequate views of God, one of which he entitles "Grand Old Man". In my mind this conjures up the image of loneliness and isolation, and I am doubly glad that the doctrine of the Trinity gives the lie to such a concept of God. Within the Trinity there is able to exist a fullness of interpersonal relationships, fellowship, communication and love between the three Persons, far richer and more meaningful than we can ever imagine. Indeed, without such interpersonal relationships within the Godhead, it is difficult to see how God could be a really personal God in His dealings with men and women. And just as the consistency within nature is a reflection of the constancy of its Creator, so the Creator's diversity-in-unity is reflected in the diversity-in-unity that we find in the ideal of marriage, and also in the universal Church which is one body, but made up of women and men, and girls and boys, purchased with the blood of the Lamb "from every tribe and language and people and nation" (Rev 5:9). We find a clear, if figurative, indication of this diversity in function in Rev 5 where we read about "Him who sits on the throne" (God the Father), the Lamb "looking as if it had been slain" (Jesus our Saviour) and the "seven spirits (or *sevenfold Spirit* signifying perfection) sent out into all the earth" (the Holy Spirit).

In closing this chapter, let us look briefly at John 14:16–26. Jesus had just emphasised both His special relationship, and His essential unity, with the Father (*"If you really knew Me, you would know My Father as well"*… *"Anyone who has seen Me has seen the Father"* …*"How can you say, 'Show us the Father'? Don't you believe that I am in the Father and that the Father is in Me?"* and, *"It is the*

Father, living in Me, who is doing His work", John 14:7, 9, 10). He then proceeds to speak about the coming of the Holy Spirit, telling His disciples, "*I will ask the Father, and He will give you* another *Counsellor* (thus like Jesus, but sharply distinguished from Him as a separate Person) *to be with you forever, the Spirit of Truth ... He lives with you and will be in you*". The Spirit comes to take the place of Jesus, yet Jesus continues by saying, "*I will come to you ... He who loves Me will be loved by My Father ... and we will come to him and make our home with him*". The Father, the Spirit and the Son are constantly shown to be separate Persons – the Son asks the Father, and in answer the Father sends another Counsellor in the Son's name (vs 26) – but at the same time their essential unity is also strongly emphasised: the coming of the "other Counsellor" is synonymous with the coming of the Son (vss 18, 20) and, indeed, with the coming of both the Son and the Father (vs 23). It would be "impossible to speak more distinctly of three who were yet one. There is a sense in which, when Christ goes away, the Spirit comes in His stead; there is also a sense in which, when the Spirit comes, Christ comes in Him, and with Christ's coming the Father comes too. There is a distinction between the persons brought into view, yet with it a common identity among them, for both of which allowance must be made" in our conception of the Godhead [35].

1. Come, Thou almighty King,
   Help us Thy name to sing,
   Help us to praise;
   Father, all-glorious,
   O'er all victorious,
   Come and reign over us,
   Ancient of days!

2. Saviour, who came to bring,
   On Thy redeeming wing,
   Healing and sight,
   Health to the sick in mind,
   Sight to the inly blind,
   O now to all mankind
   Let there be light!

3. Come, Holy Comforter
   Thy sacred witness bear,
   In this glad hour;
   Thou, who almighty art
   Now rule in every heart,
   And ne'er from us depart,
   Spirit of power!

4. To the great One in Three,
   The highest praises be,
   Hence evermore!
   His sovereign majesty
   May we in glory see,
   And to eternity
   Love and adore

J Marriott (vss 1, 3, 4) and C Wesley (vs 2, altered).

Chapter 5 : THE LORD JESUS CHRIST

We have just been reflecting on the Biblical doctrine of the Trinity, in which we came across concepts that were too deep for us to understand or imagine. To some extent, the same situation pertains to any consideration of the Person of our Lord Jesus Christ. Here we have the interplay between a human nature and a divine nature that are both complete in themselves, yet are so integrated within the Person of Jesus that He has but a single personality -- Christ Jesus the God-Man. And again, as in the case of the Trinity, we come across paradoxes created by, what is for us, an unimaginable situation, a circumstance unique in our experience. It is perhaps unnecessary to re-emphasise that Jesus was not a schizophrenic – a victim of multiple personality disorder – but the most level-headed and integrated person who has ever lived!

The Deity of Christ. We touched on Christ's deity in the previous chapter (chapter 4) when we considered the doctrine of the Trinity. However, the Deity of Christ is such an important aspect of the Christian Faith, and it is under such severe attack from many sides, that it is necessary to discuss it further. Indeed, it is probably the foundation stone of our faith – from it flows a Biblical understanding of the nature and love of God, the predicament of the human race, and God's redemption and remedy for sin.

In chapter 4 it was mentioned that the writers of the New Testament did not hesitate to apply Old Testament truths regarding *Jahweh* ("Jehovah", the LORD) to Jesus. For example, in Isaiah 6 the prophet describes his vision of the LORD, "high and lifted up", before whom the seraphim cry out "Holy, holy, holy". In John 12:41 John tells us that in that particular vision Isaiah had seen the glory of Jesus, and spoke about <u>Him</u> – thus the evangelist was linking Jesus directly with *Yahweh*. God describes Himself as *"the Alpha and the Omega"* (Rev 1:8) and as *"the First and the Last"* (Is 44:6); both these titles are claimed by the Lord Jesus Christ in Rev 22:13 and He is called the First and Last in Rev 1:17 & 2:8. In Heb 1:10 – 12 the writer quotes Psalm 102:25 – 27, a passage addressed to God, and applies it to the Son: *"In the beginning, O Lord, you laid the foundations of the earth, and the heavens are the work of your hands. You remain the same; your years will never end."*

In Heb 1:6 the writer calls on all God's angels to worship the Son, and we are given a wonderful glimpse of this actually happening in Revelation 5. Note that the Greek word used here for *worship* is the same word as that used in Luke 4:8 (*"Worship the Lord your God and serve Him only"*) and in John 4:23 (*"Yet the time is coming ... when true worshippers will worship the Father in spirit and truth"*). It is the normal word for *worship* in the New Testament. The same idea – that Jesus Christ is worthy of our worship as a reflection of His deity – is found in Phil 2:10 - 11: *"that at the name of Jesus every knee shall bow ... and every tongue confess that Jesus is Lord, to the glory of God the Father"*. Note in passing that the term *Lord* as applied to Christ is suggestive of His deity: it is the same word that is frequently used in the Greek translation of the Old Testament to designate God, and is the word commonly used in the New Testament with reference to God as "the Lord", e.g. in Luke 4:8 quoted above. Jesus is also closely associated with the act of creation (see John 1:3 and Col 1:16), and is described as Ruler over all of creation (Rev 3:14 and Col 1:15*).

We have already come across the emphatic ways in which the apostle Paul expresses the deity of the Lord Jesus Christ: He is *"our great God and Saviour"* (Titus 2:13) and *"God over all"* (Rom 9:5), and Paul expressly states (Col 2:9) that *"all the fullness of the Deity lives in bodily form"* in Jesus Christ. This is no different from the claims that Jesus made about Himself, namely *"If you really knew Me, you would know My Father as well"*, *"Anyone who has seen Me has seen the Father"*, and *"How can you say, 'Show us the Father'? Don't you believe that I am in the Father and that the Father is in Me* (John 14:7, 9, 10) **. In John 1:18 we are reminded that *"no one has ever seen God, but <u>God the One and Only</u>, who is at*

---

* Col 1:15 refers to Christ as the firstborn over all creation, implying sovereignty, priority, authority and rule, privileges belonging to the first-born in Jewish culture [36]. It does not imply *having been created*, but rather having *authority* and *pre-eminence*. Rev 3:14 may be translated as "the beginning of God's creation"; however, the sense of this verse is that Jesus is the <u>author</u> or <u>originator</u> of creation [37], "the moving cause of creation" [38] as in John 1:3 & Col 1:16. The *Watchtower* Bible (NWT) wrongly renders Col 1:16 as "by him all *other* things were created" as if Jesus is also a created being. No justification exists for inserting *other*; the Greek reads "by Him all things were created".

** Adherents of certain sects tell us that these statements refer merely to a "family likeness" and are not indicative of any deeper identity between the Father and the Son. But the import of these verses is that of both an essential unity and a special relationship (see also Chapter 4 above). Of course there would be a family likeness as well!

the Father's side, has made Him known" *. This correlates with the statements by Jesus Himself, already quoted, and is "an explicit declaration of Christ's deity" [40]. Warfield points out that this verse clearly asserts not only the full Deity of Christ, the incarnate Word, but that His Deity was not set aside by, nor during the time of, His incarnation. Thus He was perfectly fitted to be the absolute revelation of God to humankind [41].

The human nature of Christ. The discussion in the previous section has brought us to one of the other great mysteries of the Christian Faith, namely, the incarnation of the Son of God. And just as we need to approach the Being of God as Three in One with humility and wonder, so too when we consider that God became man, not in the sense of play-acting, but becoming genuinely human in all that that implies, except for sin (Heb 4:15). We can approach such a mystery only with wonder, with humility and with awe.

John the Evangelist tells us (John 1:14) that "the Word became flesh", and in Phil 2:6-8 we read that He who was in very nature God submitted to the humiliation of becoming man, even down to His very appearance – He looked like any other man – and took upon Himself the very nature of a servant. There is, we are told, one Mediator between God and men, the *man* Christ Jesus (1 Tim 2:5). The writer of Hebrews, after first establishing the Deity of Jesus Christ, tells us that *"He, too, shared in their humanity"* (Heb 2:14) and that *"He had to be made like His brothers* (and sisters – that's you and me!) *in every way"* (Heb 2:17). Jesus took part in the heritage of flesh and blood, common to all human beings, through the natural processes of gestation and birth; thus He is described as someone who is able to sympathise with our human weaknesses, and who has even experienced temptation just as we do; in other words, He was a real human being (Heb 4:15). Notice, in passing, that His was not a supernatural *birth* – otherwise He would not have been like us in every respect – but a supernatural *conception* (this is what is really implied by the "virgin birth"); thereafter his development and growth followed the normal human pattern; He was made just like us in every way.

---

* The Greek of the underlined words (page35) may be translated in various ways, such as "only-begotten God" (ANT), "God the only-begotten" (RV) and "only Son, who is Himself God" (NLT). All convey the idea that Jesus is both God and the Father's unique Son [39].

Had we been able to follow Him during those three momentous years, we would have seen Him tired, hungry and thirsty. We would have observed His tears of sorrow as He stood by the tomb of His friend Lazarus and later as He looked across the valley towards the unbelieving city of Jerusalem. We would have witnessed His agony in the Garden of Gethsemane and His intense physical suffering on the cross and, finally, we would have seen Him die. Yes, our Lord Jesus was truly human. He was not simply pretending to be a man, and so even He had need to spend time alone with His Father in prayer. We find that His knowledge was to some extent limited [as, for example, regarding the date of His "*second coming*" (Matt 24:36)]; at times He called His Father "my God" (e.g. John 20:17), and freely acknowledged that His Father was greater than He (John 10:29; 14:28). Dr R. A. Torrey [42] comments as follows: "Jesus Christ was in every respect a real man. He became so voluntarily to redeem man (*sic*) and partook of human nature that we might become partakers of the Divine nature."

There is a particular danger, current in certain theological circles, against which we must guard, namely that Christ, by becoming man, has sanctified each and every human life so that there is no longer (so we are told) any real distinction between those who explicitly acknowledge Christ and those who do not, yet show the virtues of kindness, unselfishness and concern for others, even though they might openly reject the Lord. While applauding all acts of kindness, etc, we must not lose sight of the New Testament contrast between light and darkness, nor of the solemn Biblical message of judgement upon those who reject Christ [43]. The incarnation was the starting point of God's final act of salvation, through which judgement upon all who turn to Christ in true repentance and trust would be averted, and through which He calls men and women, boys and girls, out of their darkness and into His light, to follow Him and to be His people (1 Pet 2:9).

"Tempted just as we are, yet without sin" (Heb 4:15) *. Not only do the New Testament writings contain records of temptations experienced by Jesus (Matt 4; Luke 4), they also inform us that Jesus was tempted in the same ways as we are, but that He committed no sin. He therefore understands and empathises with us in our times of temptation, and we are urged both to see in Him our

---

* I am indebted to Dr Leon Morris [44, 48] for many of the ideas reflected in this section

example of victory over temptation, and to seek strength and perseverance from Him to help us in our struggle with sin: *"Because He himself suffered when He was tempted, He is able to help those who are being tempted"* (Heb 2:18). Careful consideration of the temptation accounts reveals how signally appropriate and subtle the temptations were; yet He defeated Satan, and His victory challenges us to do the same.

In addition to the temptations recorded in the synoptic gospels (Matthew, Mark and Luke), two or three other temptations stand out very clearly: I mention but two. There was the occasion in the Garden of Gethsemane when Jesus wrestled with the temptation to give up, as His human nature shrank back from the forthcoming ordeal of humiliation, pain, abandonment and death that lay ahead. That this was a very *real* temptation (as were they all) is shown by the fact that He sweated drops of blood in His anguish of soul, and His final "your will be done" represented a victory won at great cost. The other was occasioned by the words of insult and derision hurled at Him by the chief priests and teachers of the law as He hung on the cross: "Let this Christ come down now from the cross, that we may see, and believe" (Mk 15:32). How He must have longed with all His heart for these religious leaders to turn from their hostility and doubt, and to believe in Him as Saviour and Messiah. But He resisted the temptation to come down off the cross; had He come down, there would not have been any Saviour in whom to believe!

A number of key issues arise. The temptations are important evidence for the humanity of Jesus. As already mentioned, the temptations were real temptations, and this shows, in passing, that the incarnation involved a real partaking of humanity by our Lord, and was not a case of play-acting or pretence. This links up with the idea that it was in His <u>human</u> nature that Jesus both faced and conquered temptation [45]; thus He did not "have an unfair advantage" over us in <u>our</u> struggles with temptation and sin. The only difference between Him and us in the matter of facing temptation lies in our built-in tendency to yield to temptation, whereas He was free of this bias that we call "original sin", and in His complete obedience to and reliance on His Father. This is discussed further in Chapter 6.

It is often surmised that, since Jesus was without sin, His temptations were less intense, or less wide-ranging, than those that we experience. But this is based on two fallacious assumptions. The first may be stated as follows, "that if a person does not commit certain transgressions ... it must be that he/she never felt the appeal of them" [46]. As soon as we put it like this, we realise that it is not true, even of ourselves. The second assumption is that sinlessness implies a lesser form of temptation than giving in does; that we experience real temptation only when it gains the upper hand over us. But the converse is true: the one who yields to a particular temptation has not yet felt its full power – he has given in while the temptation still "has something in reserve". Only the one who does not yield to a temptation knows the full extent of that temptation. Thus Jesus, the sinless One, is the only one who really knows temptation's full power, and knows it precisely because He did not give in, but saw it through victoriously to the end.

To think of Jesus going placidly along life's way with never a suggestion of real temptation to disturb the even tenor of His way is to empty His moral life of real worth and to exclude Him as an example for us to follow. As it is, His sinlessness resulted from His innate moral strength and from His moment-by-moment committal to the Father's will. He overcame – but it was a real victory over real temptation, won the hard way.

God-made-flesh. In the previous three sections we have looked in some detail at the deity of our Lord Jesus Christ (He is God) and at His humanity (He is man). Taken separately, these concepts are reasonably clear – we understand the concept "God" and the concept "man". But problems arise when we attempt to combine these two ideas into a single entity as the God-man; in all the universe there is no other being of whom it can be said that He is God come in the flesh (see John 1:14, 1 John 4:2 and 2 John vs. 7).

Reference was made above to the virgin birth of our Lord. This can help us to understand how God could have brought about a blend of the human and the divine in one Person: His full humanity arises from the fact of His ordinary birth from a human mother, yet His full deity was safeguarded and preserved by His conception in Mary's womb through the powerful working of the Holy Spirit. The statement that in Jesus there was "a blend of the human and the divine in one Person" is not a contradiction, but it is a paradox – a reality that we cannot fully comprehend in this age, and perhaps not in all eternity. Again, we have to make full allowance for our mental limitations when dealing with Divine realities.

Why was it necessary for Jesus to be fully human? Yes! If Jesus had not been fully human, He could not have suffered the divine judgement upon human sin, or taken upon Himself the penalty that our sin deserved. "Unless Christ was fully man ... He could not have been a substitute sacrifice for us" [47]. He could not have left us a genuine example to follow unless He was one of us, nor would we know that He truly understood our weaknesses, our difficulties and our temptations. Jesus had to be human in order to be our representative as He lived a life of perfect righteousness and obedience to God, so that we could be clothed with His righteousness by faith (Rom 3:21 – 22; Phil 3:9), and it was necessary that He be man (and God) in order to act as Mediator between God and human beings. At the same time, only Someone who is God could provide that infinite sacrifice necessary to atone for human sin – infinite, because all sin is sin against the infinite majesty of God. No finite creature, not even the most exalted archangel, would have been able to provide such a sacrifice. And only God incarnate could adequately reveal God to us so that we might come to know what He is really like, and be motivated to *"seek first His kingdom and His righteousness"* (Matt 6:33).

"Here is the ultimate mystery," writes Dr Leon Morris [48]. "Man cannot know how an incarnation is possible; it is not within his power to envisage the means whereby One who is Almighty could compress Himself within a human frame and live a human life. But we may not limit God. We take the evidence as it stands, and find ourselves affirming that Jesus was both human and divine, both God and man. Nothing less will do justice to the Biblical evidence."

Perhaps the example of the Hensel Siamese twins Abbey and Britney, born in the USA in 1991 and joined in one body from the middle spinal region down, helps us to go a little way towards accepting (if not understanding!) the existence of the two natures of our Lord in the one Person. In their case two separate individuals co-exist in (it appears) complete harmony and mutual coordination in one body, yet it points, by extension, to the possibility of two natures in harmonious fusion in one Person. The hymn-writer expressed this great Christian truth in the hymn on the next page.

1. The Son of God His glory hides
   With parents meek and poor;
   And He who made the heavens abides
   In village home obscure.

2. Those mighty hands that formed the world
   No earthly toil refuse;
   And He who set the stars on high
   A humble trade pursues.

3. He in whose sight the angels stand,
   At whose behest they fly,
   Now yields Himself to man's command
   And lays His glory by.

J-B de Santeuil

Chapter 6 : THE BIBLICAL VIEW OF HUMANKIND

We have already touched on two important aspects of the Christian view of human-ness. In the first place, human beings are God's creation – a human being is "not just a collection of chemicals that came together by an intricate process ... (our) existence is no chance or accident" [49]. We owe our whole being to God from whom all life derives – our physical abilities, our mental powers and our spiritual capacity. All our creative powers, too, derive from God our Maker. In the second place, we have already seen that we were made in the image of God: we have a will of our own and the ability to exercise freedom of choice; we have the capacity for decision-making, for love and self-giving and for the appreciation of beauty and, above all, to enter into a personal relationship with God. We occupy a position of authority, under God, over the rest of creation – we are "expected to find out the potentialities of earth, air and sea, and to use nature and its resources" [50]. Thus we can have no quarrel with the scientific quest, *per se*, which seeks to increase our knowledge and understanding of the material universe, of how it works and how it may be used for the benefit of humankind – the laws by which the world works are, after all, **God's** laws. The Bible tells us, and Science confirms, that human beings stand at the apex of life on earth, "the 'head' of creation" [51]. Science further endorses the claims of Scripture that the human race is one, derived from a single origin (Acts 17:26).

Body, soul and spirit. Theologians are divided on the question of whether human beings have a two-fold or a three-fold constitution: are we body, soul and spirit, or are we body and soul (or body and spirit) only. The Biblical evidence is not completely clear-cut, but most evangelical theologians favour a two-fold make-up for man as being overall more consistent with Biblical teaching. We know that we have a body – the material part of our being that includes the brain – and the Bible reveals to us that we also have a non-material aspect which survives death and the dissolution of the body, and awaits the Great Re-uniting at the final resurrection. This non-material part of "us" is variously described in the Bible as our *soul* or our *spirit* -- Scripture generally uses these terms interchangeably: everything that the "soul" does the "spirit" is also said to do, and *vice versa*. Thus the soul (spirit) is "the non-material element of our nature that relates to God (Ps 103:1; Luke 1:46; etc)" [52]. *Soul* also at times represents the whole person (e.g. Gen 12:5, AV).

Modern neurological (brain) research is showing more and more that our mind and emotions are very closely linked with, and centred in, the brain, and therefore, perhaps, we must regard our minds/emotions, like our brains, as part of our bodies. Recent research has also shown that the brain contains a "spiritually sensitive" area, and this tells us that our bodies too, and not only our spirits/souls, are important to God, and that we are to worship Him with both body (including mind) and soul (Mark 12:30). Such discoveries emphasise the <u>unity</u> of the person – in the past, there has been a tendency on the part of some to think of body and soul as being separated to such an extent that either may be neglected without doing injury to the other. Now we are given an added incentive to regard body and soul as a unity; neglect of one interferes with the working of the other, as is evidenced by the new approach to healing that is now known as "holistic medicine". Yet the understanding that we have a soul does not come from scientific discovery; it belongs to the invisible, spiritual realm, so our knowledge of its existence must come to us from God by revelation. For most, it will manifest itself, if at all, only in a faint, subjective perception, perhaps in what Clyde Kilby, in his anthology of CS Lewis [**53**], referred to as *the inconsolable longing*. "If I find in myself a desire which no experience in this world can satisfy," wrote Lewis, "the most probable explanation is that I was made for another world" [**54a**]. See the footnote below for two more quotations from Lewis.

So, although the Bible views the human *persona* largely as a unity in which body and soul (spirit) act together in concord and in which both are to be used in the worship and service of Almighty God, it also teaches that a time of separation lies ahead when our spirits will live on, temporarily separated from our bodies, awaiting the Final Resurrection (1 Cor 15).

Fallen man. If human beings have been created by God and in His image, it means that their lives can and should have both meaning and purpose -- a

---

* "Our lifelong nostalgia, our longing to be reunited with something in the universe from which we now feel cut off, to be on the inside of some door which we have always seen from the outside, is no neurotic fancy, but the truest index of our real situation ... We remain conscious of a desire which no natural happiness will satisfy" [**54b**].
"Our whole being, by its very nature, is one vast need; incomplete, preparatory, empty yet cluttered, crying out for Him who can untie things that are now knotted together and tie up things that are still dangling loose" [**54c**].

meaning and a purpose that ultimately come from, and are found in, our relationship with God as we commit body and soul to Him, and worship Him with both body and soul (see Rom 12:1-2). Every human being is uniquely loved by God, and he/she has the capacity to respond to that love, both in worship and service given to God, and in love and service shown to fellow humans, and especially to those in any kind of need in the world. This ideal of love and service was epitomised in the life of Jesus, whose incarnation was the example *par excellence* of self-giving and service, and shows us that in them lies meaning for us, too. He challenges us to follow His example.

The reader might well have found the preceding paragraph somewhat optimistic: real life is simply not like that! And this immediately tells us that something has gone wrong somewhere along the line, so that practice is now far removed from potential. What has gone wrong? Surprisingly, a clue is to be found in the concept of *freedom* – the freedom that God conferred upon His human creatures when He gave them free will. Just as no parents would wish for a child who always reacted like a machine with unalterable, fixed (and so predictable) responses -- responses that could never be looked upon as signs of love, because "love is the free response of an independent will and can only be voluntary" [55] -- so God, in His sovereign wisdom, endowed His human creatures with free will. This made sin possible and brought it into the human race, with all the tragic consequences that followed. And yet, as CS Lewis so cogently suggested, God "saw that from a world of free creatures, even though they fell, He could work out a deeper happiness and a fuller splendour than any world of automata would admit"; and again, "Free will, though it opens the door to evil, is also the only thing that makes possible any love or goodness or joy worth having" [56, 57].

So Adam and Eve were free to act either in obedience to God's will, or in disobedience. They chose to disobey, even though there was nothing compelling them to do so – their revolt, for that is what it was, was both deliberate and unnecessary. This act broke their relationship with the Creator and, although mind, will and emotions were affected to some extent, their main loss was spiritual, in that they lost the right to free communion with God. As Adam and Eve were our representatives, this loss has been passed on to the whole human race in a way that we cannot conceive of given the present state of our knowledge. But let's not fool ourselves. In their place we would have fared no better!

Original sin. In addition to breaking that personal relationship with God that humans originally enjoyed, we have also acquired an inherent bias towards doing what is wrong, a tendency to "go our own way". It is this that is referred to by theologians as *original sin**. In Adam humankind lost its "original righteousness" and so stands as guilty before God, and in its place gained this tendency to sin. It is inherent in our natures, manifested from an early age in such behaviour patterns as selfishness and "temper tantrums", and continues to affect all we do, so that even our best efforts are tinged with selfishness, pride and self-interest. Theologians often refer to this all-pervasiveness of sin as *total depravity* – this does not mean that we are always as "bad" as we could be, but rather that all our actions, to a greater or lesser extent, are affected by sin; that sin touches (even if ever so lightly!) everything we do. We cannot escape it. Jesus taught us that sin arises from our minds, our thoughts, our wills – in other words, that its roots are deep within us, and from there our sinful actions (individual *sins*) stem. This is so deep-rooted and so much part of us that the entire person is affected – our intellect, our desires as well as our actions. We can but agree with CS Lewis' insight, recorded in one of his delightful *Narnia* books [59]:"'You come of the Lord Adam and the Lady Eve,' said Aslan, 'And that is both honour enough to erect the head of the poorest beggar, and shame enough to bow the shoulders of the greatest emperor on earth'."

So what is sin, then? It is transgression of God's law, both His written law, and that law that is "written on our hearts" (Rom 2:15), our consciences. It is disobedience towards God and a distorting of His image within us; it is falling

---

* It was thought that "original sin" was inherited from Adam. But advances in the field of genetics have made it very difficult to think of all humankind as having been descended directly from Adam [58], and nowhere does the Bible actually claim that Adam was the ancestor of all human beings, though certain texts can be interpreted in that way. So I have chosen rather to refer to Adam ("man") and Eve ("woman") as *representatives* of the whole human race; but it is still true to say that "by one man sin entered into the world ...." (Rom 5:12). In the same way Jesus is also our representative, so that His righteousness can be credited to those who have no righteousness of their own. Sin entered the world and spread to all through the disobedience of the first Adam, our representative; righteousness came by the second Adam (Jesus, also our representative) and is available to all through faith in Him (Rom 5: 16).

short of what God intended us to be (Rom 3:23), like an arrow shot from a bow that falls short of the target and thus misses the mark; it is ultimately rebellion against God through our pride, our selfishness and our disobedience. Notice that the common feature in all these descriptions of sin is that sin is **against God**: it is an affront to God's majesty and honour, and a negation of His being, His holiness, and His sovereignty over us His creatures, and makes us subject to God's wrath, condemnation and judgement. And even when we sin against one another, in the final analysis we sin against God.

How do we come to the realisation of our own sinfulness and our need of God's mercy and grace? For Martin Luther it was his inability to find peace with God; for some, such as the prodigal son in the parable, it is a realisation of the mess that they have made of their lives; for others, it is the realisation that, like the arrow referred to above, they have fallen short of their God-given potential; and for the apostle Paul, as for many of us, it was a discovery that he was unable to do what he knew to be right coupled with an inability to prevent himself from doing what he knew to be wrong (Rom 7:21 – 23) (oh, all those broken New Year's resolutions!). JB Phillips [60] uses the illustration of a man who fancies himself as an amateur artist. Finding a blank wall, he proceeds to decorate the wall with a few sketches that take his fancy. Stepping back to admire his handiwork, he is aghast to discover that the blank wall is, in fact, part of a huge and indescribably beautiful painting that has now been spoilt by his puny efforts . . . . And that, of course, is what sin does – it spoils God's handiwork in creation, it spoils cultures and societies, and it spoils God's image in us individually and collectively. So the burning question remains, namely, *"How then can we be righteous before God? How can one born of woman be pure?"* (Job 25:4). God's answer will be dealt with in Chapter 7.

The hymn with which we close this chapter is found on page 47.

1. We have not known Thee as we ought,
    Nor learned Thy wisdom, grace and power;
  The things of earth have filled our thought,
    And trifles of the passing hour:
  Lord, give us light Thy truth to see,
    And make us wise in knowing Thee.

2. We have not feared Thee as we ought,
    Nor bowed beneath Thy holy eye,
  Nor guarded deed, and word, and thought,
    Remembering that God was nigh:
  Lord, give us faith to know Thee near,
    And grant the grace of holy fear.

3. We have not loved Thee as we ought,
    Nor cared that we are loved by Thee;
  Thy presence we have coldly sought,
    And feebly longed Thy face to see:
  Lord, give a pure and loving heart,
    To feel and know the Love Thou art.

4. We have not served Thee as we ought:
    Alas! the duties left undone;
  The work with little fervour wrought,
    The battles lost or scarcely won!
  Lord, give the zeal and give the might,
    For Thee to toil, for Thee to fight.

5. When shall we know Thee as we ought,
    And fear, and love, and serve aright!
  When shall we out of trial brought,
    Be perfect in the land of light!
  Lord, may we day by day prepare
    To see Thy face and serve Thee there.

Thomas Benson Pollock

Chapter 7 : THE CROSS, THE HEART OF THE GOSPEL

We learn from Jesus' own teaching that His death was no accident, but that it was ordained by God 'way back in the mists of eternity. Thus it was not due simply to the jealousy and anger of the Jewish religious leaders of the day or the fear that motivated a weak Roman governor. Although both of these played their part, and those involved are not absolved from their guilt for this heinous crime, a much deeper significance attaches to this event. Jesus claimed that He had come to give His life as a ransom for many (Matt 20:28), and that no one could take His life from Him, but that He had the authority both to lay it down and to take it up again (John 10:18). Indeed, an army of angels was available to assist Him had He so desired (Matt 26:53), but He obediently chose to die; otherwise no one would have had the power to put Him to death [61].

Although this chapter is headed "The cross, the heart of the gospel", it has to start, not with the cross*, but with the stable and the manger in Bethlehem, for this is where God, in the Person of His Son, entered human history, and where the final act of redemption had its beginning. It was there that Jesus first identified Himself personally with human life "in the raw" as part of God's great act of condescension, which started with the miraculous conception of Jesus as a human embryo followed by normal gestation and birth, continued with His taking upon Himself the role of a servant and culminated in His death as "He humbled Himself and became obedient to death, even death on a cross" (Phil 2:8). This process of identification involved Jesus in identifying Himself not only with human life, but with <u>sinful</u> human life as He submitted to John the Baptist's baptism of repentance -- even though He never needed to repent, nor was any sin found in Him. It was only by identifying Himself fully with fallen humanity that He could fulfil the essential function of acting as our Representative and our Substitute in God's plan of redemption.

---

* In certain quarters it is suggested that Jesus died on a "penal stake" and not on a cross; it is further maintained that a cross is a pagan symbol and has no place in Christian ritual and worship. In fact, crucifixion was used extensively for executions in the Roman Empire. Originally merely a stake on which the victim was tied or impaled, numerous pre-Christian writers confirm that by Roman times the "stake" featured a horizontal beam that, clearly, turned it into either a **T**-shape or a cross, † [62]. But does it really matter?

In previous chapters we have considered the holiness and justice of God (chapter 1) and the natural sinfulness of humankind (chapter 6). These are incompatible realities; thus it was pointed out in chapter 6 that sin is an affront to God's majesty and honour, that it is a negation of His being, His holiness, and His sovereignty over us as His creatures, and that it makes us subject to God's wrath, condemnation and judgement. So the question posed at the end of the previous chapter is one of considerable urgency and importance: "How can we be righteous before God?" The answer to this pressing question is to be found in the life and death of Christ, in His resurrection, and in the roles that He took upon Himself on our behalf, namely that of *Substitute* and *Representative*. It has already been emphasised that God's Son Jesus Christ became fully human and identified Himself completely with fallen, sinful humanity -- His birth, His childhood, His baptism, His sufferings, His death and His burial. Because of this He was competent to endure the divine judgement against human sin and the punishment that this entailed, including separation from God the Father, and death (Isaiah 59:2; Ezek 18:4; Matt 27:46; Rom 3:23; Eph 2:1). So He became our *Substitute*, bearing the penalty for our sins and our sinfulness on the cross, and bearing divine justice on our behalf, so making atonement for us. Thus God's justice has been vindicated, and forgiveness is freely available for us because Jesus has borne the full penalty for sin. Note in this connection that, since sin is rebellion against the infinitely holy God, only a sacrifice of infinite worth could atone for sin. This was accomplished in that the Victim was Himself God and thus able to present an infinite sacrifice to the Father.

At the same time, by sending His only Son, whom He loved, to bear the penalty for sin, God showed quite clearly what His attitude is towards sin: God can never again be thought of as making light of sin, and so His holiness is clearly displayed. The Son willingly accepted the role of victim, gladly laying down His life in order to make atonement for our sins; in this way, both Father and Son demonstrate the awesome love of God for His fallen creatures. Here we see God's holiness and God's love acting in concert in such a way as to emphasise the depth and intensity of each. The cross, therefore, is the ultimate display of both the holiness and the love of God, that "trysting place where heaven's love and heaven's justice meet" as the hymn expresses it.

Not only did Jesus assume the role of Substitute for us under God's judgement; He also became our Representative, again through His complete identification with the human race. Through His life of perfect righteousness and obedience to God's will, as our Representative (i.e. as "one of us"), He secured a "covering of righteousness" for us, just as if <u>we</u> had lived that perfect life -- a righteousness that is able to cover all our sins and failures in God's sight. So the apostle Paul can speak of *"the righteousness that comes from God ... which is through faith in Christ"* (Rom 3:22; Phil 3:9). Through a personal faith and trust in Jesus our Substitute and Representative, and solely because of <u>His</u> merits, we are counted as righteous in God's sight! Then, too, He represents us at God's throne in heaven where His very presence is the guarantee both of our acceptance with the Father and of His continual intercession for us as His people (Rom 8:34, Heb 7:25).

<u>Misrepresentations of the doctrine.</u> The Christian doctrine of the atonement is often misrepresented in several different ways. One such is to imply that Jesus, the innocent victim, was forced to bear the anger of a vindictive and vengeful God. But this view ignores two very important points, namely that Jesus <u>willingly</u> accepted the role of victim, and that Jesus Himself is God. Thus we read that *"God was <u>in Christ</u> reconciling the world to Himself"* (2 Cor 5:19, RSV) – the Father and the Son acting in perfect concord to effect salvation for lost humanity. In a similar vein, it is maintained that the very idea of substitution is immoral: it is charged that it would be immoral for a judge to allow an innocent victim to be sentenced to bear the punishment due to another. But once again it must be pointed out that, in this very special instance, the "judge" (God) and the victim (Jesus, Himself God) are one within the unity of the Godhead. This is not an immoral act, but the most shattering demonstration of divine love that could ever be imagined!

Then it has been quite commonly stated that the cross was all a ghastly mistake, and that God had to intervene in order to bring ultimate good out of the divine plan that went so wrong! But this is to ignore completely the sovereignty of God and the plain fact that the death of the Messiah was both foreshadowed in the Old Testament sacrificial rituals and predicted in Old Testament passages such as Psalm 22 and Is 53. Jesus is described as *"the Lamb that was slain from the creation of the world"*(Rev 13:8; see also 1 Pet 1:20): away back in the mists of eternity Jesus had already accepted the role of Saviour and all that it would cost Him! So it was not a last-minute attempt to salvage some good out of the *debacle* of Jesus' rejection by the people – it was the culmination of God's plan pre-dating the creation of the world. The wonder of it is that when evil men, at the behest of Satan and his minions, had done their worst and had done away with the Son of God (so they thought), they were found simply to have been accomplishing to the very letter God's plan decreed ages ago. The willing sacrifice was accepted, full atonement made, and Satan and his hosts exposed as a defeated foe, as shown by the mighty resurrection of Jesus from the dead and His triumphant return to the Father's glory at His ascension. Now the Father invites men and women everywhere to make this salvation their own: to accept Jesus as their Saviour, to trust in His atoning sacrifice for forgiveness, and to make Him Lord of their lives.

Let me close this chapter with the following story that I believe to be true, sent to me *via* the Internet. As it was sent anonymously, I am not able to acknowledge the original source.

> At the morning service the pastor of a Church in the USA introduced a visitor -- a retired minister -- whom he described as a special friend from his childhood, and invited him to say a few words. The old man came forward and said, "A father, his son and the son's best friend were sailing off the West coast of America. A sudden storm blew up and blocked any attempt to get back to shore, and then a freak wave washed the two boys overboard. Grabbing a rescue line, the father had only seconds in which to make the most agonising decision of his life. He knew that his son was a Christian, and that the friend was not: as he cried out 'I love you, son', he threw out the lifeline to his son's friend. By the time he had pulled the friend back to safety, his son had disappeared beneath the raging sea, and his body was never recovered.
>
> "The father", the old man continued, "knew that his son would step into eternity with Jesus, but he could not bear the thought of his son's friend entering eternity without Jesus. Therefore he was willing to give up his son to save the son's friend. How great is the love of God (he said) that He should do the same for us: He gave His only Son so that we could be saved. I urge you to accept His offer to rescue you, and to take hold of the lifeline that He is throwing out to you this morning." With that the old man sat down again as silence filled the Church.
>
> After the service, two teenagers were at the old man's side. ."That was a nice story," said one "but I don't think it was very realistic for a father to give up his only son's life on the off-chance that the other boy would

become a Christian". The old man agreed that it wasn't a very realistic thing for the father to have done. "But", he continued, "I'm with you here this morning to tell you that that story gives me a glimpse of what it must have been like for God to give up <u>His</u> Son for me. You see, I was that father, and your pastor here was my son's best friend ....."

God's "giving up" of His son was planned 'way back in eternity before the creation of the world was begun. Its implementation started with Jesus' conception by Mary in Galilee, resulting in His birth in the stable in Bethlehem on that first Christmas, and reached its culmination on the cross when the Son took upon Himself our sins. Finally, it went full circle when Jesus rose again victorious from the grave -- victorious over sin and death, and over the powers of hell itself -- and took His seat at the right hand of the Majesty on High.

Verse 1.

Hail, Thou once despiséd Jesus,
   Hail, Thou Galilean King!
Thou didst suffer to release us,
   Thou didst free salvation bring.
Hail, Thou agonizing Saviour,
   Bearer of our sin and shame,
By Thy merits we find favour;
   Life is given through Thy name.

Verse 2.

Paschal Lamb, by God appointed,
   All our sins on Thee were laid:
By Almighty Love anointed,
   Thou hast full atonement made.
All Thy people are forgiven,
   Through the virtue of Thy blood:
Opened is the gate of heaven,
   Peace is made 'twixt man and God.

Verse 3.

Jesus, hail! Enthroned in glory
   There for ever to abide;
All the heavenly host adore Thee,
   Seated at Thy Father's side:
There for sinners Thou art pleading,
   There Thou dost our place prepare,
Ever for us interceding,
   Till in glory we appear.

Verse 4.

Worship, honour, power and blessing
   Thou art worthy to receive;
Loudest praises without ceasing,
   Meet it is for us to give.
Come, O mighty Holy Spirit,
   As we hearts and voices raise;
Help us sing our Saviour's merits,
   Help us chant Immanuel's praise.

John Bakewell (altered.).

Chapter 8 : THE GOSPEL OF GOD'S GRACE

Let me remind you of the situation as it pertained in Old Testament times: the emphasis was on obedience to God's law and the performance of prescribed rituals, a system tailored by God to meet the needs and state of development and religious immaturity of the people. But even then, God looked for faith among individuals (Heb 11: 6) and for genuine repentance from those who would come to Him. Personal forgiveness was based on an appeal to God's graciousness and mercy: *"He does not treat us as our sins deserve, or repay us according to our iniquities"* (Ps 103:10), and the sacrificial system provided opportunity for confession of sin and repentance. This was really a time of preparation: God was preparing the way for the coming of Jesus, the ultimate and only true sacrifice for sin. The overall impression created, however, and so tragically illustrated throughout Old Testament history, was that the people were, with notable exceptions, incapable of obeying God's laws, or even of wanting to. So the basic question posed in Job 25:4 remained unanswered: *"How can a person be righteous before God?"*

But now, as Paul tells us, God has revealed a way of righteousness not based on obedience to a system of laws or on religious ritual, but on completely different terms -- righteousness through faith. This involves righteousness being *imputed* or *attributed* by God to those who trust in Jesus: God is pleased to *declare them to be righteous in His sight, as a gift*, despite their unworthiness and sinfulness. This is called *justification*, and exemplifies the true meaning of *grace* – the gift of God's unmerited favour, freely bestowed upon the undeserving.

The objective basis that makes this possible is the righteousness of Jesus: His life of love and perfect obedience to His Father, and His giving of Himself over to death on the cross in order to bear the divine judgement upon our sins, and to pay <u>our</u> debt of perfect obedience and love to a Holy God. Thus God's grace comes with a huge price tag – costly in the extreme to God Himself – yet it represents His free gift of love to us. What we could not do, Jesus has done for us. This is God's gift to us; in it we see the grace of God at work. We dare not make light of it, or treat it as if it is of little value, just because it comes to us free. Consider the scope of God's grace:

> God has chosen to establish a people of His own, called out of every tribe and language and nation, and invites all men and women, and

boys and girls everywhere, to become part of this special family.

He gave His only Son to take their judgement upon Himself on the cross, and so He paid the ransom-price for their sins, even though they do not deserve it.

He has forgiven their sins and cleansed them from all their unrighteousness because of Christ's finished work on the cross.

He has declared them to be righteous in His sight because their debt has been fully paid (they have been *justified*) despite their own innate unworthiness.

He has sent the Holy Spirit to impart faith and to implant God's new life in their hearts, and to be their Helper and Guide.

He has made them citizens of His kingdom, adopted them into His family, and clothed them with the righteousness earned by Christ Jesus on their behalf.

Each of these comes as a free gift and as an unmerited favour from God: each is therefore an aspect of God's grace. *The only conditions are repentance, a trust in Jesus Christ as Saviour* – thus relinquishing our trust in any other "saviour", including our own imagined goodness or moral uprightness, or even our religious observances – *and a commitment to obey Him as Lord*. This discovery has been the joyful experience of thousands of individuals, people like you and me who had/have no merit of their own, for of such is the kingdom of heaven!

No wonder that Paul rejoices in God's grace as he writes to the Christians in Rome: *"This righteousness from God comes through faith in Jesus Christ to all who believe, . . (who) are justified freely by His grace through the redemption that came by Christ Jesus."* Notice, in passing, that our salvation is not to be considered as a "reward" for our faith, because even our faith is a gift from God. Our faith is more like a "basket" that we hold out in order to receive God's gift of salvation with all its attendant blessings and privileges.

The cost of God's grace. In the previous chapter I touched on the crucifixion of our Lord. Crucifixion was a most painful means of execution, reserved only for the worst criminals. Most accounts of the Lord's suffering describe the physical suffering in gory detail: the flogging, the crown of thorns pressed into His scalp, the pain involved in being nailed to the cross, and the agony endured while waiting for death to come. But such descriptions leave out one vital aspect. We tend to forget that tens of thousands of Jews and others were crucified under Roman rule, and some of the victims endured their suffering while hanging on their cross for up to three days. So what makes the experience of Jesus so special? His physical suffering, acute as it was, was no worse than that of many other victims of crucifixion.

As I see it, the big difference is the fact that Jesus suffered the agony of separation from the Father: that was why He cried out "My God, my God, why have you forsaken me?". This marked the moment – but infinitely long in God's economy – when Jesus bore the sins of humanity. God made Him who knew no sin to be sin for us (2 Cor. 5:21), and sin separates us from God and breaks our relationship with God. As Jesus was truly bearing our real sin and guilt in order to make effective atonement for us, He would inevitably have to suffer this agony of real separation from His Father, so that <u>we</u> need never again be separated from God. It is an important, yet sadly neglected, aspect of our Lord's suffering and of His atoning love.

The abuse of God's grace. There are various ways in which God's grace to us may be abused. One is to say that, since we are saved by grace, the quality of our lives is unimportant, and we are free to live and to sin as we like. Indeed, the early Church had to counter the arguments of those who said, in effect, "the more we sin, the more grace God is able to show towards us and the greater is the glory that will accrue to His name"! Paul's scathing reply is that, in Christ, we have died to sin and been given new life in which we are united to Christ, and that this new life is incompatible with the old life of sin. To the related argument, that we might as well go on sinning since we are now under grace, so it does not matter, Paul points out that this makes us slaves of sin, whereas we are now called to be slaves of our new Lord and Master, Jesus Christ (Rom 6).

The other way in which we so easily abuse the grace of God is simply to do nothing – to accept His hard-won grace, and then to live as though it means little or nothing to us. We become Christian "couch potatoes" or "pew warmers", without realising (as we shall see in the next paragraph) that God's grace is meant to set us free for service, not in order to earn our salvation (which, of course, we cannot do) but out of a deep sense of gratitude for His love and His indescribable gift of salvation. So Jesus left us two particularly telling descriptions of the life-style that He expects us to follow: they are the Sermon on the Mount (Matt 5 – 7) and the Parable of the Sheep and the Goats (Matt 25). He also calls us to take up our cross, to share His sufferings if need be, and to be His witnesses and ambassadors in a desperately needy world.

Tragically, there are many, even ministers of the gospel, who, under the guise of being called Christian, bring the gospel of God's grace into total disrepute by behaviour that belies their profession. Such conduct might include a blatant lack of compassion, fraud, child abuse or other lewd sexual activities, etc. With God there is still forgiveness following true repentance, even for such, but the damage to Christ's cause remains.

The freedom inherent in the gospel of God's grace. Acceptance of the gospel of God's grace in Jesus Christ brings with it both peace and freedom: peace with God and with our own consciences because of the assurance that our sins have been atoned for and dealt with, and that in Christ we have been forgiven; and freedom from the imagined necessity of having to accrue merit for ourselves. Gone is the idea of having to earn our salvation, gone is the constraint of having to appease God, whether this be through religious rituals and observances, through good works, or even through our tithes and offerings. These cannot save us, and when we place our trust in them we deny the grace of God as well as the full and complete atonement achieved for us by Christ.

But when our trust is in Christ, we are set free to do these very things, not as drudgery, either out of a sense of duty or due to the constraint of a guilty conscience, but out of love for Him who, through His grace, has adopted us into His family. We are set free to do good works, to share our material possessions, and to serve God with all our energy and strength, out of love for Him who is our heavenly Father, encouraged and motivated by the love of Christ working in and through us. And, indeed, this is our calling: *"For we are created in Christ Jesus to do good works, which God prepared in advance for us to do"* (Eph 2:10). Gone for ever, too, is any excuse for boasting, since salvation is an unmerited gift given to sinners, not a reward earned by the righteous. Our only legitimate boasting may be of the merits of our Saviour – His perfect righteousness, His willing obedience, the wonder of His love. To Him be all the honour and praise.

Think of the effect of this gospel on the pagan world of the first century which was characterised by bondage to ritual, and held in the grip of fear; where lives were ruled by the stars and real and imaginary demons. Here in the Gospel was the Good News that liberated men and women from this bondage and enslavement. And in the 21st century, too, it comes as a shaft of light that has the power to challenge and dispel the darkness, the idolatry and the self-indulgence: the darkness inherent in the revived interest in the occult, horoscopes, spiritism, and Satan worship, the idolatry of materialism and covetousness, and the self-indulgence of wealth, sex and drugs.

It is into our present world that this Gospel of God's grace comes with renewed relevance, and with its ancient liberating power. Its message is simple: *Turn away from your reliance on those other things that you hope will bring you eternal life, and place your trust in Jesus only. In repentance accept God's gift of salvation, so that you may find forgiveness, and be set free to serve God and those in need in the world around you with love and compassion, and with a sense of profound gratitude. And in this find God's purpose for your life, for living.*

Tailpiece. The gospel offers us peace in our hearts and the freedom to be ourselves as God intended. But let no one think – or declare to others – that the gospel offers us a trouble-free life or a life of ease and plenty. Jesus does not bribe us with the promise of no further problems or difficulties. But He does promise that He will be with us in our difficult times, and that even they will be enriched by His presence. Committed Christians, as much as anyone else, face the daily knocks and tragedies of life, and we need to come to terms with the fact that this is the case, lest we are tempted to turn aside later through disappointment and/or disillusionment due to unfulfilled expectations.

We, too, could face the darkness of the loss of a job, or of serious financial difficulties; the darkness of a love that has gone sour, leading perhaps to the trauma of a broken marriage, of a strained relationship, or of a broken home; the darkness of illness or injury to oneself or a loved one, the aching void left by a bereavement, or the deep, deep darkness of personal depression. We are not immune. I have shared something of this darkness in others' lives, and I have experienced it in my own. I am painfully aware of the financial stress caused by an irresponsible child or unexpectedly large medical bills. I have seen the darkness produced by the break-up of a home, a shattered dream; I have seen the deep darkness caused by depression, and I, too, have shed tears over an open grave. I can testify to Christ's enriching presence in the beautiful things of life – a stable home and marriage, a sharing in the Lord's service, and children making their own, personal commitment to the Lord -- but I have experienced Christ's transforming power in my life also in the difficult times, and times of tragedy,.

1. Jesus, Thy robe of righteousness
   My beauty is, my glorious dress;
   Midst flaming worlds in this arrayed,
   With joy shall I lift up my head.

2. Bold shall I stand in that great day,
   For who aught to my charge shall lay?
   While through Thy blood absolved I am
   From sin and fear, from guilt and shame.

3. When from the dust of death I rise,
   To claim my mansion in the skies,
   E'en then shall this be all my plea:
   "Jesus has lived and died for me."

4. When the last trumpet's voice shall sound,
   O may I then in Him be found,
   Clothed in His righteousness alone,
   Faultless to stand before His throne

5. O let the dead now hear Thy voice;
   Bid Lord Thy ransomed ones rejoice.
   Their beauty this, their glorious dress
   Jesus, the Lord, their Righteousness.

Count Ludwig von Zinzendorf, (altd).

Chapter 9 : THE HOLY SPIRIT

Sadly, but with good reason, the Holy Spirit has been described as the "neglected Member of the Trinity". And certainly, the Church of the 20th and 21st centuries has known little of the Spirit's sanctifying power in individual Christian lives, or His convicting and converting power poured out upon a city or a nation. Thank God for those instances where He has been seen to be active in the recent history of the Church and of the world. But we need to start from the beginning.

The Personality and Deity of the Holy Spirit. The personality of the Holy Spirit is seen in almost every reference that is made to Him in the New Testament. For one thing, the Spirit, with few exceptions, is always referred to by the personal pronouns Him/His, not "it". This is ungrammatical as the Greek word for *spirit* (*pneuma*), is a neuter word, so that correctly (in terms of grammar) the Holy Spirit should be referred to as "It". And yet the writers of the New Testament deliberately break the rules of grammar in order to emphasise that the Holy Spirit is a *Person* and not simply an inanimate "influence" or "force".

Further, a whole host of personal activities are ascribed to Him: He teaches (John 14:26), He distributes gifts to believers according to His own sovereign will (1 Cor 12:11), He directs the missionary activity of the Church (Acts 16:7; 20:28), and He is the controlling Power behind Old Testament prophecy (2 Pet 1:21). He is active in the lives of non-believers, convicting them of sin and judgement (John 16:8 - 11), and is equally active in the lives of believers, praying for us and with us (Rom 8:26–27), cleansing us and making us holy (1 Pet 1:2) and producing His fruit in our lives (Gal 5:22f). We are urged to listen to what the Spirit says (Rev 2:7, etc), we are told not to grieve the Spirit (Eph 4:30), and we are solemnly warned by our Lord that *"anyone who speaks against the Holy Spirit will not be forgiven"* (Matt 12:32). It can be clearly seen, then, that personal attributes are ascribed to the Holy Spirit, and these cannot be explained as a mere personification of an inanimate force from God. The New Testament writers had no doubt, from their own experiences and from the teaching of Jesus, that the Holy Spirit is a Person – the One who had come to take the place of the ascended Saviour in the world, in their lives, and in their hearts.

In the New Testament there is less emphasis on the deity of the Holy Spirit than on His personality, perhaps because one of the stated aims of the Spirit was to bring glory not to Himself, but to Jesus Christ (John 16:14). Yet the writers did not shrink from applying references to God (*Yahweh*) from the Old Testament to the Holy Spirit. For example, in Acts 28:25 we read *"the Holy Spirit spoke the truth to your forefathers when He said through Isaiah the prophet..."*, whereupon there follows a quotation from Is 6:9–10 spoken by *Yahweh*, and in Heb 3:7 the works of *Yahweh* during the exodus are attributed to the Holy Spirit. In Acts 5:3–4, lying to the Holy Spirit is equated with lying to God.

Further clear evidence for the deity of the Holy Spirit is provided by the way in which we find the names of God the Father, the Son and the Holy Spirit linked together in a perfectly natural way in the New Testament. To note but three such cases:

- " ... *teach all nations, baptising them into the name of the Father and of the Son and of the Holy Spirit"* (Matt 28:19);

- *"May the grace of the Lord Jesus Christ and the love of God and the fellowship of the Holy Spirit be with you all* (2 Cor 13:14);

- *"There are different kinds of gifts, but the same Spirit, different kinds of service, but the same Lord, different kinds of working, but the same God."* (1 Cor:12:4–6).

Torrey [63] warns believers not to think of the Holy Spirit as an inanimate power that we in our weakness and ignorance must somehow get hold of and use, but rather to realise that He is a personal manifestation of the Godhead, worthy of receiving our adoration, our faith and our love, who wants to take hold of us and use us. He is not merely a gracious influence emanating from God, but an ever-present and loving Friend and Helper, infinitely wise and infinitely holy, yet infinitely tender in His dealings with us.

The work of the Holy Spirit. In discussing the personality of the Spirit, we inevitably touched on many of the functions or roles that are attributed to Him in the New Testament. He convicts non-believers ("the world", John 16:8) of their sin and of judgement to come, and reveals to them the righteousness that God has provided through Christ. He witnesses to the truth about Christ and the truth of the Gospel message (John 15:26, 27; Acts 5:32), and is the author of that new birth (*regeneration*) without which no one can be a Christian (John 3:3 - 8). It is with heartfelt gratitude and great humility that we need to remember day by day that, if the Holy Spirit had not led us to repentance, opened our hearts and minds to trust in Jesus as Saviour, and brought us to new birth, we would not have known God's salvation.

The Holy Spirit guides and directs the missionary effort of the Church worldwide, both in opening and closing doors of opportunity for missionary work (Acts 16:6, 7) and in choosing and equipping those who are to be given special tasks and responsibilities, according to His own sovereign will (Acts 13:2, 4). He empowered those first disciples to be witnesses to Christ (Acts 1:8), and He does the same today.

But it is what the Holy Spirit does in and for believers that is most often spoken about in the New Testament. The Spirit lives in believers, so that their bodies become His temples (1 Cor 6:19) – a fact that Paul uses to show the incompatibility between a Christian profession and an immoral lifestyle. Indeed, the Spirit is there to help us "put to death" the misdeeds (lusts, sinful desires and practices) of our sinful nature (Rom 8:13). We are saddled with this sinful nature till the end of our lives, but the Holy Spirit is there to help us limit and overcome its influence and to exhibit more and more clearly the fruit of the Spirit day by day, fruit such as love, joy, peace, patience, kindness, goodness, faithfulness, gentleness and self-control (Gal 5:22f) – character traits which, by and large, are often the very antithesis of the characteristics of the "world". All real beauty of character and all real Christ-likeness in us are the work of the indwelling Holy Spirit who seeks to lead us into this alternate lifestyle.

The Spirit also inspires our devotional life. He is the source of the believer's assurance that he/she is a child of God (Rom 8:16) and, casting out our fear, enables us to call God "*Abba*, Father" (almost the equivalent of "Daddy" in Hebrew), a term that expresses an especially close relationship to God of simple, childlike trust and love (Rom 8:15; Gal 4:6). The Spirit prays *for* us, but He also prays *through* us (Rom 8 :26 – 27) so that He becomes a partner with us in prayer and intercession (Eph 6:18; Jude 20), and He facilitates and enriches our praise and our worship (Phil 3:3). What an encouragement this should be for us to persevere in praise and prayer to our loving heavenly Father through His Spirit.

The Holy Spirit and the Church. The Church, also referred to in the New Testament as the "body of Christ" (1 Cor 12:12ff) and "God's household (or family)" (Eph 2:19) is the creation of the Holy Spirit, through His activity on the day of Pentecost and subsequently through the preaching of the Gospel far and wide. Believers are described as having been baptised by the Holy Spirit into the body of Christ (i.e. the Church) (1 Cor 12:13), and it is through the Spirit's action that we have been given new life and been adopted into God's family. These are synonymous statements referring to the work of the Holy Spirit as He incorporates men and women into the Church *via* the new birth, and indicate that the Church has been brought into being through the ceaseless activity of the Holy Spirit in the lives of erstwhile non-believers like you and me. It is the Spirit, too, who gives us the assurance that we are God's children (Rom 8:14ff).

Not only is the Holy Spirit the <u>creator</u> of the Church: He also <u>cares</u> for the Church. He unites individual believers, knitting them together into one body, and makes it possible for them to enjoy spiritual fellowship with each other. He also acts to unite the body of believers in a real, but mystical, union with its true Head, Christ (Col 1:18). He is the **Holy** Spirit (Rom 1:4), and as such works towards the sanctification both of individual believers, and of the Church as a whole, to the glory of God (Rom 15:16; 1 Cor 6:11).

As further evidence of His care of the Church, the Holy Spirit equips individual believers with spiritual gifts to be used for building up and strengthening the Church (1 Cor 12:7; 14:12), and the apostle Peter urges that *"each one should use whatever gift he has received to serve others, faithfully administering God's grace in its various forms."* Every member of Christ's body has been given some spiritual gift as an evidence of the Spirit's working in his/her life, gifts that are intended to be used for building up the local Christian community and not for selfish advantage or self-glorification. The gifts that are given are many and varied, from the high-profile gifts of leadership in the Church (apostles, prophets, pastors and teachers) (Eph 4:11); to gifts that might be used to enrich public worship or pastoral care (such as the ability to speak words of wisdom or knowledge, the ability to perform miracles or healing, faith to meet a specific need, the gifts of discernment, prophecy or tongues) (1 Cor 12:8–10); and finally to the "behind-the-scenes" gifts that might appear rather mundane but are still very important, such as the ability to encourage others, to show mercy, to be of service to others, and to be able to contribute to the financial needs of those in need (Rom 12:6ff). We also read about "helps" and those who have the gift of administration – often, and wrongly, considered a rather "unspiritual" gift.

In the light of some recent teaching about the gifts of the Spirit, some further comments would not seem out of place. This has become an area of controversy within the Church, especially the gift of *tongues* because of the publicity it has received. I do not have the gift of tongues myself, but I have no problem with the fact that many Christians, including many of my friends and acquaintances, do have this gift. However, I do have a problem with those who suggest that *all* Christians should speak in tongues, or (alternatively) that those who speak in tongues are more "spiritual" or more favoured by God – that they, and they alone, are the first- class Christians. This is a totally unscriptural notion.

For one thing, the Spirit gives the gifts sovereignly, just as He wills. And in his letter to the Corinthians Paul specifically asks, "Are all apostles? Are all teachers? Do all work miracles? Do all speak in tongues?" The implied answer in each case is "no". The whole point about these spiritual gifts is that the Church has need of them all (including the less spectacular gifts mentioned above), and so different gifts are given to different members of the Church for the good of all.

Recently, I have again been thinking about the incident regarding Cornelius (Acts 10). You will remember that Peter had a vision of "unclean" animals to prepare him for an urgent invitation to visit the home of a Roman centurion – a Gentile. So Peter accompanied the messengers to Cornelius' home, and on his arrival he told the Gentiles who had gathered there about Jesus. And while he was still speaking to them, the Holy Spirit came upon all who heard his message and they (the Gentiles) spoke in tongues and praised God (Acts 10:44–46). What I realised as I thought about it was that my conversion, and yours, were as genuine as that of Cornelius & Co, but the Spirit seems to have planned different gifts for many of us, perhaps because their situation and their particular needs in the 1st century are not the same as our needs in the 21st century.

Then, too, we sometimes hear it said that the gifts of the Spirit, including the gift of tongues, are so little in evidence in the Church to-day because we are not expecting to receive them. But if you read Acts 10:4 you will see that neither were the Gentile listeners nor Peter and his companions: they were all amazed at what had happened. This brings us back to the Biblical truth that the gifts of the Spirit are entirely under His sovereign control, and are distributed as He wills, as He sees the need. They are given for building up the Church and its believers, and they are not meant either as a source of pride ("see what I have!"), or as a reason for jealousy ("I haven't, and I want"). We have all been given gifts. What gift(s) have *you* been given to help build up the Church, I wonder?

The Spirit has come in His fullness and has been poured out upon believers in order to lead us into God's truth and to guide us in our service for the Master, to give us His gifts which are to be used in building up the Church, to produce His fruit in our lives as He shapes and moulds us, and to empower us to evangelise the world.

The believer's responsibility. In his letter to the Philippians Paul writes, *"work out your salvation with fear and trembling, for it is God who works in you to will and to act according to His good purpose"* (Phil 2:12–13). Rightly understood, this is not in any way a denial of the gospel of grace, but a timely reminder of the believers' responsibility to be co-workers with God in their own spiritual development and that of the Christian community (Church) to which they belong. God is not glorified by those who refuse to take responsibility for their own growth or that of their fellow believers! And so it is, as we close this chapter on the Holy Spirit, that we must be aware of <u>our</u> responsibility *vis-à-vis* the Holy Spirit's work in us and in our growth towards holiness. Our responsibility in this matter has both a positive and a negative aspect.

Positively, we must ensure that we are *"filled with the Spirit"* (Eph 5:18). The Greek present tense is used to indicate that the filling with the Spirit is not a once-for-all experience. Repeatedly, as the occasion requires, the Holy Spirit empowers for worship and for service [59]. The early disciples were initially filled with the Holy Spirit (Acts 2:4) and, when persecution started, were filled again (4:31) as they pledged their continued allegiance to Christ's cause. The original Greek here is rich in meaning, and suggests that believers should both be filled *with* the Spirit, and also that the Spirit is the agent through which our lives are filled – thus both *with* the Spirit as well as *by* the Spirit. Little wonder then, if the Holy Spirit fills our lives with Himself, that we should become springs of living water (John 7:38) in a thirsty world.

What does it mean to be filled with/by the Holy Spirit? It means being under the Holy Spirit's control to such an extent that He directs our thoughts, feelings, words and actions. It means constantly leaving our lives open to His influence upon them, and so to "experience in the fullest measure the indwelling and the enriching presence of the Holy Spirit" [64]. It requires dedication and commitment to God of the highest order. And, because of our innate frailty, we have to be ever watchful that we do not gradually drift back into self-will or indifference, and so drift away from the Spirit's influence and control over our lives. Thus the duty is laid upon us of seeing that we receive in full measure – and again and again – the filling and the fullness that only God's Spirit can bring. We are told to be filled with/by the Holy Spirit; in other words, even though the Spirit's coming is a gift from God, the responsibility is laid upon us to facilitate, from our side, this wonderful privilege of having God's Holy Spirit on board as Captain! How can this become true in our own lives? Morris [65] shares the Biblical teaching with us in the following terms.

In the first place, we need to *ask* for the gift of the fullness of the Holy Spirit. The Lord Jesus stated clearly that our heavenly Father gives the Spirit to those who ask Him (Luke 11:13). Such a request clearly implies a deep desire to receive this precious gift from God -- Jesus likened it to a thirst for something better in life (John 7:37). And we must ask in *faith*, believing that God hears us.

The second condition is *repentance* – and repentance means, "being sorry enough to quit", and so goes far beyond mere confession. Yes, if we are to share in the Spirit's fullness, we must be willing to confess our sins and failures, but we must also be willing to turn our backs on every sinful action and tendency in our lives: thought, word and deed. We cannot expect the Spirit's fullness if pride or selfishness rules our lives, or if pornography has a hold upon us, or if we defraud the Receiver of Revenue (to give but a few examples at random). The gift of the Spirit is for those who repent and obey God (Acts 2:38; 5:32).

But let both be wholehearted – a wholehearted renouncing of sin, and a wholehearted obedience to God. Morris recounts the story of a little boy whose hand got stuck in the neck of a valuable vase. His father tried repeatedly to pull the boy's hand free, but to no avail. In one last attempt, the father said to his son, "Hold your fingers out, quite straight, like this, and then pull." "But I can't do that, Daddy", his son replied. "If I did, I'd drop my penny!" Sadly, we Christians often hold onto our penny (or cent) so firmly that we miss out on the riches and freedom of the Spirit's fullness.

Turning again to our responsibility in the matter of the Spirit being active in our lives, we have considered the positive responsibility of seeking the fullness of the Spirit. But there is also a negative side: we are warned neither to *grieve* the Spirit (Eph 4:30) nor to *quench* the Spirit (1 Thes 5:19). What do these warnings mean for us in practice? How do we grieve or quench the Spirit?

All sin grieves the Holy Spirit. But in this context, grieving the Holy Spirit appears to be specially connected with not maintaining a loving relationship with others, particularly fellow Christians: when this is <u>not</u> done, the Spirit is grieved. So our anger and/or resentment towards one another, our unkind words and actions, and our critical attitude towards each other, grieve God's Spirit and rob us of our joy in the Lord. The Spirit is the bond that unites us with one another in fellowship within the body of Christ, and "the sin of offending a brother (*sic*) by false word or act especially grieves Him" [66].

We are warned also not to *quench* the Spirit, a highly appropriate metaphor when we remember that the Holy Spirit came upon the early disciples in the form of flames of fire (Acts 2:3). Commentators disagree as to how exactly to interpret this warning, some linking it with sin in one's personal life, others linking it particularly with anything that militates against freedom and spontaneity in the service of worship. It would seem to me best simply to take it at face value: do not do anything that will put out the fire of the Spirit in your life, for example by harbouring known sins or wrong attitudes, or by gradually drifting away from the Lord through neglect either of His word or of time spent in His presence (or both). As our commitment wanes, so our enthusiasm evaporates, our hearts grow cold, and the Spirit's fire in our lives is effectively quenched.

Conclusion. In concluding this rather brief and inadequate chapter on the Holy Spirit, it is perhaps necessary to emphasise two matters of special importance. The first of these is that the Holy Spirit is indeed God, and not a vague, impersonal force or power that happens to be on the side of "good". He is the third member of the Trinity, equal in majesty, holiness and glory with the Father and the Son, and comes to us with all the authority of God. However, we must not separate the members of the Godhead into three distinct beings or "gods": when the Holy Spirit comes to us, the Father and the Son come in and through Him, and "we have access to the infinite divine resources of God Himself" [67].

The other equally important point is that the fullness of the Spirit is not meant for a few chosen super-Christians! God longs for, and expects, *every* Christian to experience His fullness, His power and His holiness in their lives. The gift of the fullness of the Spirit is available to all believers in order to draw them closer to God, to deepen their joy in the Lord, and above all to equip them more effectively for service, to the glory of God the Father.

Finally, let us remember that, no matter how much of our lives the Spirit may control, there will always be other areas where we have not yet allowed Him to have sway. As Stibbs & Packer point out [68], "the extent to which the Spirit actually penetrates and possesses every moment of our time, every corner of our lives and every sphere of our thought and activity, is always capable of enlargement". Let us make every effort, with the Spirit's help, to yield more and more of our life's nooks and crannies to Him day by day.

1. For Thy gift of God the Spirit,
    With us, in us, e'er to be,
  Pledge of life, and hope of glory,
    Saviour, we would worship Thee.

2. He who in creation's dawning
    Brooded o'er the pathless deep,
  Still across our nature's darkness
    Moves to wake our souls from sleep.

3. He it is, the living Author,
    Wakes to life the sacred Word;
  Reads with us its holy pages,
    And reveals our risen Lord.

4. He, the mighty God, indwells us
    His to strengthen, help, empower;
  His to overcome the tempter –
    Ours to call in danger's hour.

5. He it is who works within us,
    Teaching rebel hearts to pray;
    He whose holy intercessions
    Rise for us both night and day.

6. In His strength we dare to battle
    All the fiery hosts of sin,
    And by Him alone we conquer
    Foes without and foes within.

7. Fill us with Thy holy fullness,
    God the Father, Spirit, Son;
    In us, through us, then, for ever,
    Shall Thy perfect will be done.

Words: Margaret Clarkson
© 1960 Hope Publishing Co., Carol Stream, IL 60188.
All rights reserved. Used by permission.

Chapter 10 : THE CHURCH: ITS NATURE AND RESPONSIBILITY

It is appropriate to look at the doctrine of the Church immediately after considering the Holy Spirit, since it is the Holy Spirit who gives believers their new life, and unites them in fellowship with one another in this common life that they all share. So it is the Spirit who unites believers in that one body which we call "the Church" – hence Paul can tell the Corinthians (1 Cor 12:13) that *"we were all baptised by one Spirit into one body, whether Jews or Greeks, slave or free "*. Thus the Church is a creation of the Holy Spirit, and consists of all those who acknowledge Christ as Saviour and Lord, whatever their race, occupation, age or social standing might be. The Church Universal includes present believers and all those who have died "in Christ" in the Christian era, as well as God-fearing believers from the time of the Old Testament, one community over whom Christ is Lord and King. So in a very real sense the Church is a continuation of the 'people of God' of the Old Testament, and as such can rightly be referred to as *"the Israel of God"* (Gal 6:16)*.

The Church is visible yet invisible. Many of the epistles of the New Testament were written to specific local congregations – groups of believers of which the membership was known. It is the same today: local congregations consist of members whose names appear on the Church or parish membership roll or baptismal register. And even where no formal records are kept, it is quite clear who is and who is not associated with that congregation. The sum total of all those who have such a visible affiliation with a local Church worldwide, as well as those deceased who in their lifetime had such an affiliation, make up what is called the visible Church: the visible Church is the Church as it is seen on earth, and is one aspect of the Church Universal.

---

* But, you ask, what about Gentiles who never heard about the God of the Hebrews: is there any hope for them? And what about the billions alive today who have never heard of the love of God and of Jesus the Saviour? I can only speculate! In Matt 25: 31 - 46 Jesus spoke about the sheep and the goats, and the final separation at the last judgement. But it is the **nations** that are gathered before the judgement seat – in Jewish terminology, the Gentiles. Are these, possibly, the people who have never heard of the true God? Will they be judged in accordance with the criteria that Jesus outlines: not whether they had faith in Him (which they could not have had), but how they treated those in need around them? (Read that passage yourself, and meditate on it, for surely it tells us how the Lord wishes us to live, too!)

But there is a second, paradoxical, aspect that must be considered: the Church is also <u>invisible</u>. In its true spiritual reality as the fellowship of all genuine believers, the Church is invisible. We cannot see into the hearts of professing believers, or judge anyone's spiritual condition. Only God can do that, and the Scriptures tell us that *"the Lord knows those who are His"* (2 Tim 2:19). Its membership is not recorded with complete accuracy in the combined membership rolls of all local congregations, but only in *"the Lamb's Book of Life"* (Rev 21:27). The invisible Church is the Church as God alone sees it, and includes isolated believers in places where there is no local Church as such. There must, clearly, be a considerable overlap between the memberships of each of these two aspects of the Church Universal, yet they are not identical.

In the New Testament we find mention made of many who were members of the visible Church but who showed, by their later attitudes, that they were not members of the invisible Church. Paul writes of a certain Hymenaeus "who has made shipwreck of his faith" (1 Tim 1:20); later (2 Tim 2:17f) Paul describes how this same Hymenaeus, aided and abetted, it seems, by one Philetus "has wandered away from the truth ... and is destroying the faith of some". Others, too, are mentioned by name, and Paul warns that from within the local Churches teachers would arise who would speak perverse things in order to draw believers away from the true faith (Acts 20:29f).

In His series of parables recorded for us in Matthew 13, Jesus compared the Kingdom of God both to a farmer's field, initially planted with good seed, in which an enemy sowed noxious weeds, and also to a dragnet that caught both good fish and bad. In each case an ultimate separation of the good from the bad took place. These parables foreshadow and picture the two aspects of the Church that we have just been discussing: the visible Church being a mixture of both true believers and others, whereas the invisible Church is composed of the true believers only. Here is also a warning for each one of us – to make sure that our faith is genuine and that our commitment to Jesus is real.

The Church is both local and universal. In the New Testament the word *Church* may be applied to groups of believers of any size, from a small house-Church (e.g. Rom 16:5), to all the believers in an entire city such as in Corinth (1 Cor 1:2) or in a much larger region, such as *"the Church throughout Judea, Galilee and Samaria"* (Acts 9:31). The word is applied to the Church throughout the entire world (and, indeed, down through the ages), the Church

Universal (e.g. Eph 5:25). But let us not forget that Jesus promised that where even two or three believers only were meeting in His name, there He would be in their midst (Matt 18:20). And surely where Jesus is meeting with His followers, there is the Church, even if only in embryo. So we conclude with Grudem [69], "the community of God's people considered at any level from local to universal may rightly be called by the name '*Church*'."

The nature, calling and purpose of the Church. The New Testament uses a number of metaphors to describe the Church. Some implicitly suggest different possible forms of ministry, and will be dealt with in the next section; others imply aspects of the Church's calling and character. For example, the Church is likened to the branches of a vine, where Christ Himself is the "trunk" of the vine. This speaks to us about the all-important need to allow His life and strength constantly to flow into us, and challenges us to remain in a close relationship with the Lord so that we may be able to produce fruit, "for without me", He said, "you can do nothing" (John 15:5). Another metaphor is that of a building, of which Christ is the cornerstone – that stone "which determined the design and orientation of the building; (it) was the most important stone in the structure" [70]. Jesus is the cornerstone, and in Him believers are united together as the smaller stones built into the walls (1 Pet 2:5f). The same is true of the metaphor that depicts Christ as the Head of the body (Col 1:18): it speaks of Christ's authority and control over His Church, and of the unity between its members as well as their individual uniqueness and diversity. The Church is "the family of God", challenging us to love and care for one another (2 Cor 6:18) and the "bride of Christ", a metaphor that calls us to purity, both of life and of doctrine (Eph 5:32; Rev19:7).

The purpose of the Church may be stated quite simply as a four-fold calling to minister, as follows [71]:

(a) **Ministry to God: Worship.** The Church is called to be a worshipping community, praising God for His goodness, bowing in adoration before His majesty and holiness, and ascribing to Him the glory that is due to His name (Ps 29:2). Our lives, too, must be lived to the praise of His glory (Eph 1:12). This is discussed further in chapter 11.

(b) **Ministry to believers: Nurture.** The Church is called to help each member to grow both in love and in the understanding of his or her faith, to build them up and to enable them to "grow in grace and in the knowledge of our Lord Jesus Christ" (2 Pet 3:18). God has distributed spiritual gifts – in the form both of gifted persons (Eph 4:11) and of special abilities (1 Cor 12:8ff) – so that the saints (you and I!) may be equipped for service and that the whole body of believers may grow towards Christian maturity (Eph 4:14f). And of course the goal of evangelism (see below) is not simply to bring individuals to salvation, but to lead them on into true discipleship and Christian maturity.

(c) Ministry to the world: Evangelism. It is significant that the last recorded utterances of Jesus have to do with evangelism, as for example the "great commission" (Matt 28:19f) and parallel passages at the end of Luke and at the beginning of Acts, emphasising the importance of evangelism in the Lord's thinking. Thus the Church is urged to spread the Christian gospel to the people of every land and nation, starting with Jerusalem and Judea, then Samaria and so on to the ends of the earth. Sadly, at many times of its history, and for many centuries, the Church lost this vision of her Lord and dilly-dallied while men and women, boys and girls, lived and died without even hearing about Jesus. Is it not the same to-day? Many local congregations are so involved in survival strategies that evangelism is very far from their minds. But this is, in a sense, a vicious circle, because the Church or congregation that has lost its evangelistic vision is in any case unlikely to survive. The responsibility laid upon each one of us is to use every opportunity to share Jesus with others, and to take an interest in, and to support as best we are able, initiatives that seek to spread the gospel, whether within our own nation or farther afield.

(d) Ministry to the world: Socio-political upliftment. Jesus made it clear that His kingdom was not to be a political kingdom that would compete with the kingdoms and empires of the world; rather, it was to be a spiritual kingdom with spiritual goals, expanding by spiritual means. Nevertheless, it was to be a kingdom that had a social conscience, a kingdom whose citizens would be concerned about the needs of others, even of non-members: a kingdom where, for example, the untouchables of this world would be embraced, where the unloved would find love, where children would be taken seriously – where they could be both seen and heard! -- and where the poor would be invited to share in the riches of Christ as well as in the material wealth of the more fortunate.

It is clear that the Church has, by and large, failed to live up to her Founder's example and teaching. Not only have both her worship and her evangelistic effort become tainted with hypocrisy, but Christians who have been called to show acts of mercy, of kindness and of love whenever the need arises and it is within their power to do so have fallen very far short of their Lord's teaching and example; we have grieved the Holy Spirit, and have given the world the opportunity to denigrate our Saviour and the gospel that we proclaim! So we are challenged to repent of our lack of love, and to follow our Saviour's example of unconditional love and service in the power of His Spirit.

Models of ministry. Three New Testament passages e– John 10, 1 Cor 12 and 1 Peter 2 -- have this in common: each of them provides the basis for a particular "model" of ministry within the Church at local level. Let us briefly look at each model in turn.

(a) The shepherd - flock model. In John 10 we read about Jesus as the good shepherd: the sheep follow Him, and He lays down his life for his sheep. This has given rise to the so-called "shepherd-flock" model of ministry and is what many would see as the "traditional" model. A shepherd (the minister) is appointed to lead the flock (the congregation); the flock pays him, and he gives of his time, his energy and his wisdom, often selflessly and sacrificially, in the interests of his flock. He has the training, experience, and skill, and is the undisputed leader of the flock: he leads, and the flock follows his lead.

This model has significant disadvantages, however. A congregation structured upon this model might well expect the minister to do everything, and the members can easily become rather passive followers who are often not prepared to share responsibility for the life and activities of the Church. They make demands upon the minister, and they feel cheated if these demands and expectations are not met to their satisfaction: "Why does he not start a Bible study group?" "I wish the minister would start a prayer meting"; "Why does he not visit us more frequently?" etc. In short, they (the congregation) will follow the lead that the shepherd (minister) gives, provided <u>he</u> organises the programme and does the visiting. It also assumes that one person – the minister – will have a multitude of gifts: preaching, pastoral care, administration, teaching and evangelism, etc. Many ministers, too, assume that they, as the shepherd, must do everything themselves, and allow little real scope for lay involvement in the spiritual side of the Church's ministry.

Such a model, whilst it might meet the needs of a fledgling congregation in the middle of the first century, or of a Church made up largely of young Christians at the start of the 21st century, does not encourage growth towards Christian maturity. It stands or falls by the personality, the gifts and talents, the energy, enthusiasm and effort of the minister. Little wonder that so many ministers reach burn-out or suffer nervous breakdown in the course of their ministry, and why the members fail to grow up into Christian maturity. I came across the following apposite comment in the Magazine of the Presbyterian Church in Ireland: "Crucially, we need to dispense with the outdated model of 'a performing clergy and a receiving laity' and get back to the Biblical model of an every-member ministry" [72].

(b) The Body-of-Christ model. Paul's favourite picture or image to represent the Church is that of the "body", found in 1 Cor 12, where it is described in some detail. So we look, in the second place, at what is generally called the *Body-of-Christ* model. In such a congregation each member is looked upon as an individual with particular gifts, talents, and also limitations. Each is expected to play a part in the life and work of the Church: members are encouraged to exercise their gifts to the full, each member is recognised as having a unique contribution to make, and opportunity is provided for individuals to contribute and grow. The minister occupies a more modest position: his role is less that of a leader and more that of a guide or a facilitator who provides opportunities for service and ministry, and so helps the members to grow in maturity as they are able to exercise their various gifts and to take greater responsibility, since each member has a part to play in the functioning of the body as a whole.

But there is a danger of the worship becoming rather subjective if it is too often allowed to emphasise the subjective feelings and experiences of the worship leader(s) as opposed to objective Biblical truth. The congregation also needs to be on its guard against subconscious spiritual pride that could give rise to a first-class-versus-second-class spiritual mentality based on the spiritual gifts that members are perceived to have or not to have (as touched on in Chapter 9). Both subjectivity and spiritual pride must be firmly resisted.

(c) The priesthood-of-all-believers model. A third model that seems to be little recognised, but fits in well with the doctrinal position of reformed Churches, is encapsulated in the words of Peter the apostle: *"But you are a*

<u>royal priesthood</u>, *a holy nation, a people for God's own possession, that you might declare the wonderful deeds of Him who has called you out of darkness into His marvellous light*" (1 Pet 2:9). This same idea is found in Rev 5:10 "*... purchased men for God from every tribe and language and people and nation, and ... made them a kingdom and <u>priests to our God</u>*". So we consider as our third model what might be entitled the *priesthood-of-all-believers* model.

I am often amazed -- indeed, concerned and saddened -- by the expressions of surprise I receive when people, including fellow Church members, discover that I regularly conducted services at a local Mental Hospital on behalf of my Church. It seems inconceivable to many that a layman should do this. I also find myself saddened when friends of mine suggest, in all seriousness after I have prayed with them about some need or concern, that I clearly have a special, direct line to heaven. [Have you come across this too?] My answer is usually, "Yes, I <u>do</u> have such a direct line -- but it's a line that is open to all in Christ; that it does not depend on me and <u>my</u> merits, but on what Jesus has done, on His merits; <u>He</u> is my direct line". Are we not told in Heb 10:19-22 that the shed blood of Jesus gives us a *"new and living way"* by which we (<u>**all**</u> Christians) are able to draw near to God?

It is experiences such as these that convince me that my third model of the Church is both little known and little understood by Christians and non-Christians alike: many people appear not to see any further than our first model, namely the Shepherd-flock model, and it is inconceivable to them that anyone other than the shepherd is equipped to do anything for God! Peter tells us that **<u>we</u>** are "a royal priesthood"(1 Pet 2:9), and it is my concern that local Churches and their members should now start living this out in practice. The Old Testament priest formed the <u>bridge</u> between God and the people; he functioned in both directions, God-ward <u>and</u> man-ward, presenting the people's needs to God, and bringing God's blessings to the people. Now the New Testament tells us that we are <u>all</u> royal priests -- priests who serve the King of Kings – and we have the duty and privilege of ministering to one another in the congregation as well as to those who are still outside of Christ. You will notice that we are now moving beyond individual gifts, helpful and necessary as they are, to a privilege and a responsibility laid upon us all to be God's representatives both in the world and towards members of our own congregation.

Allow me to give you just a couple of examples from my own experience as I have sought to be a priest, in the sense I have outlined above, in my everyday professional life. I remember sitting in a car and praying with a fellow teacher who was worried and upset about a wayward daughter, and how grateful she was for my concern. I recall praying for a fellow elder right there on the pavement outside the local post office where I met him as he wrestled with a difficult decision. And I remember visiting a colleague who was very seriously ill, and praying for her healing -- and how she told me months later that that had been a turning point in her attitude towards her illness!

We can <u>all</u> become involved in this kind of informal ministry as opportunity offers, and in so doing we can begin to fulfil more completely our Lord's command to love one another. There are risks attached, of course. There is the (true) story of a Christian businessman who, hearing that a colleague's wife was ill, asked if he could "lay hands on her", only to be told in no uncertain terms that if he so much as dared to lay even one finger on the wife he would be severely beaten up!! More seriously, it took me months to get over my frustration and anger that God had not seen fit to heal a friend for whom I had prayed. Yet God challenges us to accept the risks and to exercise this Biblical privilege of ministering informally as His priests whenever we are aware of a particular need that we can address in the name of Jesus. This model, based on the concept of the priesthood of all believers, contains within itself scope for <u>all</u> God's people to exercise ministry. We can't all preach or teach, but we can all listen to others, we can all share with others, and above all, we can all pray for and with others in their need (or joy).

The Bible presents this model in the contexts of worship within the assembly of God's people (Rev 5:9-10), reminding us to exercise our priestly function to the benefit of our sisters and brothers in Christ when we meet together for worship. It also presents it in the context of proclamation to the world (1 Peter 2:9, 12), thus urging us to be God's priestly ambassadors in our daily lives "out there" where the need is so great, to the glory of our.

Thinking about it, perhaps *vision* would be a more appropriate word in this context than *model*. What is <u>your</u> vision for your local Church and how it should function? And what part can you play in its life and work, both within the assembly of God's people and in the broader community 'out there'? May the Holy Spirit give you a vision towards which you can strive.

The communion of saints. This phrase comes from the "Apostles' Creed", a statement of faith which was first attested in 380-381 AD [73]. This particular phrase is not found in the Scriptures, and it is difficult to find any scriptural proof for some of the more extravagant ways in which it has been interpreted. The "Apostle's Creed" reads as follows: "I believe in the holy universal ('catholic') Church; the communion of saints; the forgiveness of sins; and the life everlasting. Are we saying that we believe that we can commune with deceased believers or with those recognised by the Church as "saints"? But note that the word *"saints"* is the ordinary Biblical word for ordinary Christians such as you and me, as for example *"Paul .... to all the saints in Christ Jesus at Philippi"* (Phil 1:1).

An obvious interpretation of this clause in the creed appears if we assume that there is a comma, and not a semicolon, after the word "Church", so that the statement reads: "I believe in the holy universal Church, (which is) the communion of saints; the forgiveness of sins; and the life everlasting". The sense now is that it is within the Church that believers ("saints") enjoy communion or fellowship. But there is some doubt as to whether this was all that the original compilers of the creed intended to convey by the phrase "the communion of saints".

One can go a step further and point out that, all down the centuries since New Testament times, there have been common rites performed -- as for example the Lord's Supper and the use of the Lord's prayer -- so that Christians through the ages have shared in this common heritage and in these common practices, giving a feeling of solidarity (or "communion") with fellow Christians separated by distance and/or by time. And finally, one can point out that when we worship we join with the worship that is already taking place before God's throne in heaven, a paean of praise from the whole Church, "militant" as well as "triumphant" (Heb 12: 23). Perhaps those who have gone before us sense our worship mingling with theirs, and rejoice in it.

As far as I know, there is no Biblical evidence that we are able to contact, and thus have direct communion with, the departed saints – that would be akin to spiritism, and is roundly condemned in the Bible. Nor is there any suggestion that they are able to see us or to know anything about us, and there is not even a hint that we are able to pray to any departed saint, whatever connotation we might give to the term "saint". Although Heb 12:1

tells us that we are surrounded by a great cloud of witnesses (referring particularly to the "heroes" of faith from Old Testament times who have gone before), the Greek implies that it is their <u>example</u>, recounted for us in Scripture, that should inspire us to persevere when we feel like giving up [74], rather than that they are actually watching us as we fight our own spiritual battles here on earth or that we may look to them for help.

1. Lord, her watch Thy Church is keeping;
    When shall earth Thy rule obey?
 When shall end the night of weeping;
    When shall break the promised day?
 See the whitening harvest languish,
    Waiting still the labourers' toil;
 Was it vain, Thy Son's deep anguish?
    Shall the strong* retain the spoil?

2. Tidings meant for every creature,
    Millions still have never heard!
 Can they hear without a preacher?
    Lord Almighty, give the word!
 Give the word, in every nation
    Let the gospel trumpet sound,
 Witnessing a world's salvation
    To the earth's remotest bound.

3. Then the end: Thy Church completed,
    All Thy chosen gathered in,
 With their King in glory seated,
    Satan bound, and banished sin.
 Gone for ever parting, weeping,
    Hunger, sorrow, death and pain;
 Lo! Her watch Thy Church is keeping:
    Come Lord Jesus, come to reign.

Henry Downton

* "the strong" here refers to Satan (see Matt 12: 26–29, especially vs 29).

Chapter 11 : WORSHIP

The word "worship" is often used very widely to describe all the activities that take place at, for example, a Sunday "worship" service. But much that takes place is not, strictly speaking, worship, however important it might be. I am using the word in a more restricted sense in this chapter, namely that worship refers to that aspect of a Christian's devotional life in which we bow before God because of who He is, and in our innermost being give Him the glory that is His due while we lift our hearts (and voices) before Him in reverence and praise. So worship, in this sense, is our response to God's majesty and greatness, to His holiness and love. Clearly, this refers both to corporate worship as believers together, and to our personal worship when we spend time alone in God's presence contemplating His glory. Both are vitally important for the Christian.

Many scriptural passages speak to us of God's indescribable glory and majesty, and so often give the impression that the prophet is groping for words to describe the indescribable, and incomprehensible, glory and holiness of God. In Ezekiel's vision (Ezek 1) we read of flashing lights, of an awesome layer ("expanse") of what looked like sparkling ice crystals, a sapphire throne, a rainbow -- a veritable kaleidoscope of colour -- and of an appearance like fire and glowing metal from which Ezekiel hid his face (have you noticed how workers in a gold refinery wear goggles in order to cut out the glare?). If this is a vision that includes much of a purely symbolic nature, what must the awesome reality itself be like? And the prophet Jeremiah speaks to us of God's greatness and power in the following terms: *"But the Lord is the true God; He is the living God, the eternal King. He made the earth by His power, He founded the world by His wisdom, and He stretched out the heavens by His understanding."* I am grateful that modern Science amplifies and extends our view of the universe, and so confirms and enlarges our vision of the majesty of God. His greatness and power, His wisdom and understanding are far beyond our comprehension. Christians – and, indeed, all who believe in the Creator-God -- should become increasingly aware of, and increasingly excited by, the way in which Science has magnified these aspects of God's nature and Being for us.

It is fitting, therefore, that in our approach to God we should come with a sense of awe and wonder: awe and wonder as we think of His greatness, holiness, majesty and love. It is fitting that we should come to Him reverently, in adoration and worship, and with praise in our hearts and on our lips. So when we come to God in prayer, whether corporately (with other Christians) or simply by ourselves, let us spend time in giving Him the honour, the glory and the praise that are His due as God Almighty. Sadly, this aspect of Church life is often conspicuous by its absence, especially perhaps in the "non-conformist" Churches. We need to realise afresh that not only is God our <u>Father</u>, but also that our Father is <u>God</u> – with all that this implies. Here I appeal to any who read these pages and who also have the privilege of leading others in worship: do make sure that <u>this</u> "ingredient" of reverent adoration and heartfelt wonder at God's majesty is not neglected, either in the prayers you use or in the hymns you choose, and do spend time thinking prayerfully of new ways in which a congregation may be drawn more fully into sharing in true spiritual worship.

The importance of worship. What, then, is the importance of worship? For one thing, it is God's due simply because He is God. *"Who should not fear (revere, honour) You, O King of the nations, for this is Your due ... there is none like You."* (Jeremiah 10:7). It is also true that God is looking for people who will enter into such a worshipful relationship with Him that He might pour out His blessings upon them: *"The time is coming* (said Jesus) *when the true worshippers will worship the Father in spirit and truth, for they are the kind of worshippers the Father seeks"* (John 4:23-24). Furthermore, worship meets one of humankind's deepest needs: we were made to have fellowship with God and to walk humbly before Him, and worship both strengthens our relationship with God and shows us our frailty in the light of His glory and majesty. It has been well said that in <u>supplication</u> we are thinking about our needs and the needs of others; in <u>thanksgiving</u> we are focusing on our blessings; and in <u>confession</u> we are concerned with our sins. But in <u>worship</u> we focus upon God Himself. Where worship is neglected, or has been allowed to become very formal, God will remain small and ineffectual, purely the creation of our own finite minds. But this is not the God of the Bible, the Lord of all creation and sovereign Ruler of the universe!

Private worship. In our own private worship we can use verses of hymns or portions of Scripture to articulate our thoughts as, like Ezekiel, we attempt to give expression to the indescribable glory of God, as we try to imagine the unimaginable greatness and majesty of His power and holiness. I give but a few examples from Scripture that I have found helpful:

- *"You are the high and lofty One, who inhabits eternity, whose name is holy"* (Is 57:15)
- *"Great is the Lord and greatly to be praised; His greatness is unfathomable"* (Ps 145:3);
- *"Holy, holy, holy is the Lord God Almighty, who was, and is, and is to come"* {Rev 4:8);
- *"Worthy is the Lamb who was slain, to receive power and wealth, wisdom and might, honour and glory and blessing."* (Rev 5:12, RSV),

God welcomes us into His presence as we come to meet with Him, in Jesus' name, in praise and worship. But let us come into His presence with reverence, with humility and with awe as is fitting when we approach Him who is the Almighty Creator and the Ground of all Being. And if our worship is preceded by a time of stillness in which we bow before God in quietness, with a mind and heart that are silent before Him, simply waiting quietly in God's presence, He will reveal Himself to our souls. Indeed, do the Scriptures not tell us to *"be still, and know that I am God"* (Ps 46:10; see also Ps 37:7) and again *"The LORD is in His holy temple: let all the earth be silent before Him"* (Hab 2:20)? We will find that God makes Himself known to us in our inmost being: He will flood our souls with the sense of His presence, and our hearts will be lifted up in deeper and richer worship, adoration and praise. (This, surely, is the Christian answer and antidote to the cult of "Transcendental Meditation" that has become so popular in the western world since the early nineteen sixties!)

I remember vividly a story entitled "The Great Stone Face" that I read as a ten-year-old at school:

> A young boy, growing up in a village in the foothills of the Andes Mountains, used to spend many hours contemplating an unusual rock formation high up on a cliff face. When the sun shone on it at a particular angle, the weathered rocks took on the likeness of a human face -- a serene and peaceful face, humble yet strong. Legend had it that, at some time in the future, a man would arrive in the village bearing the likeness of the Great Stone Face. As he contemplated its beauty and strength, the young boy prayed that he would live to see the coming of this legendary man.

He grew up to become (in his own words) a humble preacher. One evening towards sunset as he was speaking to a small crowd in the market place, there was a sudden stir among the people who had gathered to hear him. Then the cry went up "the Great Stone Face has appeared at last" -- and, lo and behold, the people were pointing to <u>him</u>, the humble village preacher...!

Need I say more? As we spend time with God in worship, in contemplation of His power and glory, His holiness and majesty, not only does His power flow into us, but we are also gradually changed into His likeness. As the late Dr. Torrey wrote [75] "Beholding God, and worshipping God, we become more like God". The writer of a modern hymn expressed the same thought when he wrote:

> Beholding Him, until my face his glory,
> My life His love, my lips His praise shell tell.

<u>The heavenly worship : a pattern for us to follow?</u> Chapters 4 and 5 of the book *Revelation* give an evocative description of the worship that is taking place in heaven, and I ask myself, "is this perhaps an example that we can follow, is it perhaps a pattern for our own worship, both as individuals and when we come together as a congregation of God's people?" These passages give us three major motives for worshipping God, and we would do well to take heed of them for our learning.

The first of these is founded upon <u>the nature of God's being</u>. Here we have a reminder of His holiness and power: "*Holy, holy, holy is the Lord God Almighty*" is the cry of the living creatures around the throne. We also have a reminder of His eternity: "*Who lives for ever and ever … who was, and is, and is to come*", and we have an indication of His sovereignty: God is depicted as seated upon His throne, the King who creates according to His sovereign will – and we hear an echo of this as the heavenly beings cry out, "*… by Your will they were created and have their being*". They worship God because He is holy, eternal, and the sovereign Ruler of the universe -- King both of time and of eternity.

In the second place, notice that the heavenly worship also focuses on <u>God's act of creation</u>. *"You are worthy"* they call out, *"for You created all things, and by Your will they were created and have their being."* As a scientist, I believe that the very properties of the atoms and molecules that make up the universe, the forces that hold them together, and their characteristic patterns of behaviour, have been decreed and designed by God in order to achieve His purposes, that life itself might ultimately develop and flourish wherever He willed it. So I find myself, again and again, echoing the words of the prophet Jeremiah (already quoted above): *"God made the earth by His power, He founded the world by His wisdom, and He stretched out the heavens by His understanding."* It is our privilege to worship the sovereign Creator-God, all wise and all powerful.

And then, thirdly, the heavenly worshippers extol <u>God's act of redemption in Christ</u>. The focus now (Rev 5) shifts to the theme of salvation as they see *"a Lamb, looking as if it had been slain, standing in the centre of the throne"* -- a poignant representation of our Lord Jesus, reminiscent of the Passover lamb and echoing the prophetic words of John the Baptist, *"Behold, the Lamb of God!"* His appearing ushers in a new song, a new motive for worship: *"You are worthy because You were slain, and by Your blood You purchased men and women for God from every tribe and tongue and people and nation, and have made them a kingdom, and priests to serve our God"*.

Who are those who cry out "Worthy is the Lamb who was slain"? Rev 5:11 tells us that they are angels – thousands upon thousands of them – who encircle the throne in order to worship the Lamb. His sacrificial death was such a stupendous act of self-giving and love that the angels raise their voices in praise to Him. But He did not die for them -- He died for us! So how much more should <u>we</u> not lift our hearts in praise and worship to the Lamb who once was slain? The hymn-writer expressed it as follows:

> *"Worthy the Lamb that died they cry, to be exalted thus;*
> *Worthy the Lamb, our lips reply, for He was slain for us."*

It is perhaps appropriate to introduce a sombre note at this stage, lest we forget the horror associated with the unfolding drama -- the Lamb would have been depicted with its throat cut (*"as if it had been slain"*). This picture of a sacrificial Lamb in heaven tells us something more about God: not only of the great love He has for us, but also that He takes sin very seriously. The fact that the Lamb had to be <u>slain</u> for us tells us *that God could not simply overlook sin as though it did not matter.* It would be contrary to His nature, and contrary to that holiness about which we have already been reminded, for Him simply to overlook sin. God's holiness and justice demand that sin should be shown to be what it really is, and that it had to be fully and finally dealt with before we could be accounted righteous in His sight, and before we could really worship

Him in spirit and in truth. Our worship should remind us, time and again, of how serious a matter sin is, and how infinitely costly it was for God the Father, and for Jesus our Lord. Let us never, ever again, treat sin as if it did not matter. If only we could see sin, in all its ugliness and shame, from God's perspective and through His eyes….

But let us return briefly to the heavenly worship as depicted for us in Rev 4 and 5. We note that the heavenly worship is "balanced" – the multitude before the throne worship both "Him who sits upon the throne" as well as "the Lamb" (Rev 5: 13). In my own experience in various Churches, too often the worship in hymn and in prayer focuses only upon the Lamb, our Saviour Jesus. We would do well, both in private and in communal worship, to follow the balanced pattern shown us in heaven.

There is one detail that has not yet been touched on, and it is this: the elders, as they worship, "*lay their crowns before the throne*" of God. [The Greek here denotes victors' crowns, like those given to athletes. Jesus promised such crowns to all who persevere in their faith and finish their spiritual race (Rev 2:10)]. These crowns are the most precious possessions they have! Yet they are willing to give them up, glad to lay them before the throne as an offering to God. It speaks to me of what Paul wrote to the Romans (Rom 12:1):"*Therefore I urge you ... to offer your bodies as living sacrifices, holy and pleasing to God, which is your spiritual worship*". At the same time, the Bible speaks about offering to God "a sacrifice of praise" (Heb 13:15). Now a sacrifice requires a victim, and the 'victim' associated with the sacrifice of praise can only be our pride and self-will. As we worship and praise God, these must be offered to God, put to death, and burned (Heb 13:11)! This, the offering of ourselves and our most precious possessions wholly to God, is the only proper response to worship that is offered "in spirit and in truth", and is itself part of that worship. This echoes the words of the hymn-writer:

> "Changed from glory into glory,
> Till in heaven we take our place;
> Till we cast our crowns before Thee,
> Lost in wonder, love and praise."

So we are called to worship our God, not only by raising our voices in praise to Him, and by lifting our hearts in adoration before His throne, but also by presenting ourselves as living sacrifices to Him, to be used in His service. Like

Moses after he had spent time in God's presence on Mount Sinai, may our faces, and our lives too, shine for God in this needy and hungry world as we spend time worshipping in His presence, and then go out to do His will in service that is an adequate reflection of our worship.

1. With gladness we worship, rejoice as we sing,
    Free hearts and free voices how blessed to bring.
   Our praise and our worship shall scale Thine abode,
    Thou King of all glory, most bountiful God.

2. Thy right we would give Thee -- true homage Thy due,
    And honour eternal, the universe through,
   With all Thy creation, earth, heaven and sea,
    In one acclamation we celebrate Thee.

3. Renewed by Thy Spirit, redeemed by Thy Son,
    Thy children revere Thee for what Thou hast done.
   O Father! Returning to love and to light,
    Thy children are yearning to praise Thee aright.

4. We join with the angels, and so there is given
    From earth "Hallelujah" in answer to heaven.
   Amen! Be Thou glorious below and above,
    Redeeming, victorious and infinite love.

G Rawson

Chapter 12 : THE COVENANT

God enshrines His will for His people, and the corresponding blessings and promises, in terms of what are often referred to as *covenants*. And generally each covenant also stipulates the responsibility that that particular covenant laid upon God's people – that is, God's covenants are generally <u>conditional</u>. We will confine our attention to three major covenants (or rather, three different expressions of the one eternal covenant), but first we need to consider an overview of the history of redemption.

Brief overview of the History of redemption. We are all familiar with the story of Adam and Eve however we may interpret it, and notice there the beginnings of a conditional covenant. The blessing promised was unrestricted fellowship with the Creator; the condition was obedience to the single, testing command that God gave them. We know that they failed the test, and sin was let loose into the world, to be passed on through Adam, as the representative of mankind, to all future human beings, as is so clearly depicted in the chapters of Genesis that follow. Although this was not unforeseen by God, it meant that the emphasis would now shift towards redemption, whereby God could establish a people for His own possession (Is 43:21; 1 Pet 2:9).

God now revealed Himself as the *calling, choosing* God: He called Abram out of the idolatrous cities of Ur and Haran, in both of which the moon-god was worshipped [76], and chose him to be the forebear of a new nation. Then, successively, God chose Isaac and Jacob from whom this new nation, God's people Israel, would descend. But this was not an end in itself: the ultimate goal was to prepare the way for the coming of the Saviour – the Redeemer, the Messiah – through whom God's kingdom would be established and through whom the concept "people of God" would be broadened so as to include not only the faithful out of Israel, but also Gentiles from every nation on earth. To this end God chose Mary, a young woman from Nazareth, to be the mother of Jesus, God's only Son come in human likeness, the long awaited Messiah and the long-promised Saviour. And down through the ages God has been calling to men and women and inviting them to become members of the people of God and citizens of His kingdom.

Each major step forward was marked by a divinely instituted covenant, although the word *covenant* is not completely appropriate. Such covenants were not simple agreements, but expressions of the Divine will to which the other party in the covenant, for example the nation of Israel, was called upon to commit themselves. As mentioned previously, each such covenant included promises of blessing attached to a specific condition (or set of conditions), so that, in a sense, they were more like *testaments* that expressed the will of God for His people without any possibility of negotiation. And surely the Sovereign Lord of the universe has the right to act in this way, however one-sided it might seem to be to us!

The three covenants. The essential element at the heart of the covenants that God has made with humankind – the "core blessing" – is the promise "I will be your God, and you shall be my people" (e.g. Jer 31:33). But in each case, as already noted, this promise is conditional. Let us look at three of the most important covenants, namely that with Abraham, with the people of Israel through Moses, and the New covenant initiated by our Lord Jesus Christ, but anticipated by the prophets Jeremiah (31: 31-33) and Malachi (3:1).

In the **Abrahamic** covenant God promised to be Abraham's God and the God of his descendents, and that through them all the nations of the earth would be blessed, upon the condition of total consecration to the Lord as symbolised by circumcision (Gen 17:1-11; 22:17-18). The **Mosaic** covenant was a divine pledge to be Israel's God – her protector and the Guarantor of her blessed destiny -- on condition of the nation's continued consecration to God as their Lord and their King, to live as a people under God's rule and to serve His purposes in history. The rite of circumcision remained the sign and the symbol of the Mosaic covenant (Ex 19:5,6), but instituting the Sabbath was an additional reminder of the covenant. The code of laws that formed part of the covenant stipulations included criminal, civil and ceremonial laws that acted to restrain the sins of the people [**76**], regulated their worship, and were a constant reminder to the people of God's holiness and their special calling to be different from the surrounding nations.

The **New** covenant (Luke 22:20), also referred to by Jesus simply as "the covenant" (Matt 26:28), and represents both a fuller revelation and a wider application of God's grace than could have been known or understood previously. It is founded on the death of Jesus who, on the eve of His crucifixion, said of the cup at supper "this is my blood of the covenant, which is poured out for many". The covenant is thus ratified by the blood of Jesus shed for the sins of the world and sealed to individual believers by the operation of the Holy Spirit (Eph 1:13; 4:30), and fulfils, at least in part, the promise of God through the prophet Jeremiah*

What, then, are the promises and conditions of this covenant? These are spelled out throughout the New Testament, as for example in John 6:35,40: *"Jesus declared, 'He who comes to me will never go hungry, and he who believes in me will never be thirsty. For my Father's will is that everyone who looks to the Son and believes in Him shall have eternal life, and I will raise him up at the last day'"*. The <u>promises</u> include having our spiritual hunger and thirst satisfied, and receiving the gift of eternal life with the pledge of final resurrection. The <u>conditions</u> include *coming to Jesus, looking to the Son* and *believing in Him*. These phrases, which are largely synonymous, speak to us of true commitment, a living faith in Christ, and trusting in the efficacy of His blood, shed as an atoning sacrifice for our sin.

The sign or symbol of the new covenant is Christian baptism, which symbolises, i.a., the washing away of sin through the blood of Jesus. Baptism has now replaced circumcision as the sign of the covenant: circumcision involved the shedding of blood, pointing forward to the death of Jesus, whereas baptism, which does not involve bloodshed, points back to that same event in which Jesus, once and for all, shed His blood for the forgiveness of sins. The question of baptism is dealt with in chapter 13.

All three covenants – that with Abraham, with the people of Israel through Moses, and the new covenant in Jesus Christ – are covenants of *grace* in that the almighty and holy God graciously stoops to establish a relationship with fallen human beings, offering them His blessing and inviting them to become a holy nation, His own special people in whom He will live and among whom He will walk, and making them sons and daughters of their heavenly Father (2 Cor 6:16,18). This blessing finds its present fulfilment in the Church, the people of God (however distorted the reality may be), but it will find its ultimate fulfilment in the new heavens and the new earth in the age to come (Rev 21:3).

---

* "This is the covenant I will make with the house of Israel after that time", declares the Lord. "I will put my law in their minds and write it on their hearts. I will be their God, and they will be my people. ... For I will forgive their wickedness, and will remember their sins no more" (Jer 31: 33-34).

Thus we may think of our relationship to God, both individually and corporately, in terms of this new covenant, giving us an added sense of security in our relationship with Him since we know that this relationship is based on a set of promises that He will never change, the only condition being continued trust and commitment to Jesus Christ. This new covenant is the eternal covenant in Christ, through whom the faithful shall forever have fellowship with God: He will be their God, and they will be His people [77].

1. All praise to God who reigns above,
   The God of all creation,
   The God of wonders, power and love,
   The God of our salvation.
   With healing balm my soul He fills,
   The God who every sorrow stills –
   To Him all praise and glory!

2. What God's almighty power hath made
   His gracious mercy keepeth;
   By morning dawn or evening shade
   His watchful eye ne'er sleepeth;
   Within the kingdom of His might,
   Lo, all is just and all is right –
   To Him all praise and glory!

3. The Lord forsaketh not His flock,
   His chosen generation;
   He is their Refuge and their Rock,
   Their Peace and their Salvation.
   As with a mother's tender hand
   He leads His own, His chosen band –
   To Him all praise and glory!

4. Then come before His presence now
   And banish fear and sadness;
   To your Redeemer pay your vow
   And sing with joy and gladness:
   Though great distress my soul befell,
   The Lord, my God, did all things well –
   To Him all praise and glory!

Johann J Schütz

Chapter 13 : BAPTISM

When I was a university student in the late 1950's, the major point of discussion within the Christian Union was the question of baptism: whether infants could/should be baptised, or whether baptism should be restricted to believing adults only. Interestingly, the different points of view that were expressed never caused a rift amongst us – merely some light-hearted banter! Yet the discussions did point up the underlying differences of opinion on this important issue current in the various Churches represented on the campus at that time.

Perhaps it is appropriate at this juncture to clarify one small matter about baptism, and it is this: neither the baptisms that John the Baptist administered, nor the baptism of Jesus in particular, can rightly be considered to be _Christian_ baptisms. John's baptism was a baptism of repentance to prepare the way for the coming of the Lord. And Jesus' own baptism was an act of solidarity and identification with fallen humanity, in preparation for His earthly ministry and His death on the cross for the sins of the world. _Christian_ baptism is in the Name of the Trinity, and follows Jesus' commission to His disciples to go into the world to preach the gospel and to make disciples out of every nation.

The New Testament teaching on Christian baptism. Like John's baptism, baptism as practised by the early Church, and as interpreted by the apostles, also emphasised repentance. But its overall significance was far broader. Analysis of the New Testament texts reveals that baptism in the New Testament symbolised (i) Christ's redemptive work, that is, that Christ has died for me, (ii) my response in faith, as shown by my repentance and commitment; and (iii) God's application of the benefits of redemption to my life, in that I have been given new life in Christ through the Holy Spirit. Thus baptism was clearly a picture of purification and new life, and pointed to the fact that "the blood of Jesus Christ cleanses us from all sin" (1 Jn 1:7). But it is only a picture or a symbol, it does not accomplish these blessings for us – it is a picture of what God does in the life of every believer. The teaching on baptism in the New Testament assumed that those who were baptized were already believers: that they had already come to faith in Jesus, repented of their sins, and committed their lives to Him. In such cases, baptism is a symbol of death to the old life, and rising to a new life in Jesus (Rom 6: 4 – 7).

What, then, about the common practice of administering baptism to infants? Is there any support for this practice in the New Testament? Some find support in the scattered references to the baptism of "families" or "households", the assumption being that these families or households must have included infants as well as adult believers (Acts 16: 14-15; Acts 16:34 and 1 Cor 1:16). However, as Grudem has shown [78], upon careful analysis these references do not provide unambiguous supports for infant baptism *.

Upon reflection, it is perhaps not surprising that the New Testament says nothing specifically about infant baptism. We know, as has been pointed out by Motyer [79], that the New Testament Church was a first-generation Church and none of the examples of baptism recorded in the New Testament relates to an adult who had grown up within the visible Church -- all came to Christ from non-Christian (including Jewish) backgrounds.** The situation now is totally different; can we really expect the New Testament to speak directly to such a changed situation? What we do have is a record of our Lord's attitude towards young children: He took them up in His arms and blessed them, saying, *"Let the little children come to Me, for the kingdom of God belongs to such as these"* (Luke 18:16); He rejoiced that the Father had revealed spiritual truths to little children (Luke 10:21); and He used a little child as an

---

* Another presumed supporting text for the practice of infant baptism is Acts 2: 39, where Peter declares that "the promise is to you and to your children". But as the verse continues "*... and to all who are far off*", it seems more likely that he was speaking about future generations rather than referring specifically to young children then alive.

** Cunningham [80] has shown quite clearly that even the reformed Confessions of Faith like the Heidelberg Catechism and the Westminster Confession had adult (believers') baptism in view, and that the statements made there about baptism apply to adult baptism only, and cannot be applied directly to infant baptism. He writes, "infant baptism is to be regarded as a subordinate thing ... which cannot well be brought within the line of the general abstract definition or description of a sacrament, as applicable to adult baptism and the Lord's Supper. The Westminster divines, then, have given a description of a sacrament, which applies fully to adult baptism and the Lord's Supper, but which does not directly comprehend infant baptism."

example to all would-be disciples, coupled with a dire warning to anyone who damaged such a child's faith (Matt 18:2ff). All are agreed that Jesus had a very soft spot for little children, but is there any warrant in Scripture for actually baptising infants and young children?

Baptism and circumcision. In chapter 12 we had a brief look at the theology of the covenant, and saw that circumcision was the divinely appointed sign or symbol both of the covenant that God had made with Abraham and also of the covenant that He made with the nation of Israel through Moses. But we also saw that, come the Christian era, the sign* of the covenant was changed from circumcision to baptism (Col 2:11-12), a rite that does not involve any shedding of blood, and which can be applied alike to males and females.

Since circumcision was commanded to be administered to infants, it would seem to be both permissible and logical under the new dispensation for infants to be baptised. This, of course, does not in any way negate the practice of baptising adult believers – in the Old Testament we find examples of both adult [for example, Abraham (Gen 17:10-11)] and infant circumcision. Is there any reason, then, why <u>both</u> forms of baptism should not be practised in the same denomination and in the same local Church, so long as it is accepted that baptism in the Name of Father, Son and Holy Spirit, whether adult or infant, is (like circumcision) a once-and-for-all rite, valid for a person's whole life?

Although all Israelite males were circumcised, and so were marked with the sign of the covenant, it is clear that many of them, possibly the majority, turned out to be *covenant breakers*: they were numbered among God's covenant people and so should have been heirs of God's covenant promises, but they did not fulfil the conditions that God had set, namely their continued consecration to God as Lord and King, to live as a people under God's rule, and to serve His purposes in history. They went astray after idols, desecrated the Sabbath, and neglected their appointed festivals and holy days. But there was a small minority (a remnant) who <u>did</u> keep the covenant conditions; they are described in both Old and New Testaments as being "circumcised in their hearts" (e.g. Deut 10:16; Jer 4:4; 9:26; Rom 2:29); elsewhere Paul points out

---

* I hesitate to use the term "seal" in this context, despite its use in the Westminster Confession (Article 28), as neither circumcision nor baptism are referred to in Scripture as "seals" of the covenant. Believers have been sealed with the <u>Holy Spirit</u> (Eph 1: 13; 4:30).

(Rom 9:6) that *"not all who are descended from Israel are* (true) *Israel"*. So physical circumcision was given as the sign of the covenant that God made with Abraham and his descendants, but it looked for its fulfillment in the circumcision of the heart. Only such as were circumcised in their hearts were God's true covenant people, the real (spiritual) Israel.

We can surely apply analogous reasoning to the situation of the Church *vis-à-vis* baptism: the sign of baptism looks for its fulfillment in the baptism of the Spirit (1 Cor 12:13), also called regeneration or the new birth ("being born again") (John 3:3). Baptism makes us members of the visible Church (see Chapter 10), whereas through the new birth we become members of the invisible Church, the people of God under the new covenant, and inheritors of the riches promised us in Christ. This is true whether we are thinking of infant baptism or of believers' baptism, though in the case of adult believers, baptism is a sign of the new birth that they have already received {just as circumcision was a sign to Abraham of the righteousness that he had already received through faith (Rom 4:11)}. The Old Testament analogy suggests to us that God, in His wisdom, decreed that the whole process of leading a child in the way of truth and righteousness is best accomplished within a family, and that it should start right at the beginning of his little life. So to-day, when a Church baptises the baby of parents who want _their_ precious infant to grow up in the way of Christ, and have confessed their own faith in Christ in the presence of the congregation, that congregation is affirming its belief in the biblical principle that "Christianity begins at home" [81]. Of course, this is true only when parents are serious about maintaining a truly Christian home.

The meaning and significance of baptism. It is important that in any discussion on the meaning and significance of baptism we do not nullify – or even appear to nullify – the clear teaching of Scripture that salvation comes to us by and through God's grace alone: *"By grace you have been saved, through faith, not by works"* (Eph 2:8-9) and *"I do not set aside the grace of God, for if righteousness could be gained through the law, Christ died for nothing"* (Gal 2:21). We must be clear ourselves, and the Church must make it clear to all who come for baptism, or to their sponsors (e.g. parents), that one is not saved through or by baptism, lest we spread false hopes and give encouragement to those who do not feel the urgency of their need to come to personal faith in Christ. Sadly, baptismal liturgies tend to convey the impression, especially to parents who bring their infants for baptism, that a baptised person will be saved* whether or not they have been born again or, alternatively, that baptism is to be equated with, or automatically produces, the new birth. **

Baptism signifies that the person who has been baptised is a member of the covenant community, the visible Church, just as circumcision signified membership of the Old Testament covenant community, the nation of Israel. But just as circumcision looked for its fulfilment in the circumcision of the heart, so baptism looks for its fulfilment in the baptism of the Spirit, the new birth. Some object to young children, who have not yet made a personal commitment to the Lord, and might never do so, being included in the covenant community. But we remember the attitude of our Lord Jesus towards young children, and Paul's statement that the children of believing parents, or even of only ONE believing parent, are holy and so are rightfully members of the covenant community until such time as they choose otherwise, either through outright rejection or through apathy and indifference.

Both modes of baptism symbolise the cleansing power of the blood of Christ and forgiveness of sins in His name. Believers' baptism looks back to regeneration already having happened in the life of the baptised person and symbolises being united with Christ in His death and rising with Him in newness of life (Rom 6:3-4), a realisation that, for many Christians, will grow with time. A Church service at which a baptism of this nature takes place can be a very moving experience. The act of being baptised because one has made a decisive commitment to trust Jesus as Saviour and to crown Him as Lord of one's life is something very special; it can be a source of great encouragement, and often seems to make the reality and the wonder of Christianity come alive.

---

* In 1 Pet 3:21 we read that the flood and Noah's ark are a picture of "baptism, which now saves you" (NLT). But Peter deliberately points out that it is not the outward physical act, but the inward spiritual reality that baptism represents, namely identification with Christ and transformation through the power of His resurrection, that saves us from God's judgement upon our sins.

** For example, a recent revision of a denominational Confession of Faith stated that in baptism "the Holy Spirit acts to unite us to the Lord and so to wash away our guilt, give us new life in Christ, ordains us into the priesthood of all believers and commission us to serve the risen and ascended Lord." Although this might be symbolized in *believers'* baptism, it is highly misleading (unless further amplified) when applied to the baptism of infants.

Infant baptism, on the other hand, looks ahead to this becoming a reality in the future, not because of the rite of baptism itself but through the response of faith to the call of God that issues in a personal commitment to Christ. Parents of baptised infants need to pray fervently, and with great perseverance, that this will occur in their own child's experience and, as they will have promised, to ensure a loving and explicitly Christian home for their children. Perhaps it is fair to say that believers' baptism symbolises commitment to Christ as Saviour and Lord, whereas infant baptism symbolises the love that God has for children by incorporating them into the covenant community and inviting them to become committed followers of Christ when they are old enough to make such a decision for themselves. It also reminds us of the dire warnings aimed at any who cause a child to stumble. So infant baptism emphasises God's gracious invitation to all concerned to come to Christ, and challenges members of the congregation to ensure that they have really committed their lives to Christ and trust Him as Saviour, whereas in believers' baptism the baptised person testifies that he or she has already made that commitment.

The effects of baptism. Since the Church has been commanded to baptise, and since any act of obedience to the Lord carries with it a measure of blessing, we would expect the practice of baptism to be accompanied by blessing for both the Church and its members. Believers' baptism is specifically a public act, usually made within the congregation, that involves confessing and witnessing to the reality of Jesus as Saviour, and this in itself brings joy to the believer and to the congregation, and results in a mutual strengthening of their faith. Through baptism the Holy Spirit challenges the believer to live out more and more fully, in the power of the Holy Spirit, both his/her death to the potency and love of sin, and his/her resurrection into new life in union with Christ (Col 2:12-13). Thus baptism "becomes a 'means of grace' through which the Holy Spirit brings blessing to the person being baptised and to the Church as well" [82].

And now we can attempt to answer the question, "What does infant baptism accomplish?" Again, as an act of obedience, infant baptism, rightly administered, will be a blessing to the Church. It symbolises the cleansing power of Christ's blood, and the Holy Spirit will use this symbolism as a means of proclaiming the love of God and of strengthening faith. It assures the Church of God's love for children, challenges her to take children as seriously as Jesus did, and incorporates the children of believers into the visible Church. Baptism certifies that they are members of the covenant community so that they come under the promises, as well as the obligations, of the covenant of grace. As such, baptised children should be accepted as real members of the Church family where their spiritual welfare will be an important priority for the whole Church; where they can be taught and come under the sound of the gospel; and where they will be encouraged to commit their lives to Christ when they are able to decide their spiritual future for themselves. The act of baptism calls attention to the fact that, by sending His Son, God took the initiative in our salvation, and in baptism the Church claims the children for Christ and receives them into its fellowship [83].

As we have seen, the act of baptism is a picture, for all who witness it, of God's way of forgiveness and cleansing through the blood of Christ. As such it presents a challenge to all baptised persons (through the Scriptures faithfully preached and the working of the Holy Spirit) to respond appropriately in repentance and faith, lest their own baptism remains an empty sign and does not find its fulfilment in conversion and the new birth (see Deut 10:16 and Jer 4:4). One could even say that baptism should evoke a longing, amongst all who witness the rite, to put their own lives right with God (Deut 30:6).

Who are appropriate subjects for baptism? We have already seen that, in the New Testament Church, all the unambiguous instances of baptism involve those who had already (prior to their baptism) turned to Christ and were able to make a clear profession of personal faith in the Saviour – and this despite mounting opposition and persecution! In this sense, baptism is a symbol of beginning the Christian life, and so is administered to those who have already started out on their journey with Christ; this is the basis of believers' baptism, with which we can have no quarrel. But it was also pointed out above that the New Testament Church was, by its very nature, a first-generation Church, and those who joined it were converts out of Judaism or paganism. I have tried to show that there is a scriptural alternative, based on the divinely appointed practice of circumcision, which applies in a situation such as we have today where babies are born into Christian families that are already members of long-established Churches. The New Testament is totally silent regarding the practice of baptism under such conditions, even in the established Churches of the day such as Corinth, Ephesus and Philippi, although we do know that proselytes to Judaism were baptised as a sign of their new-found faith, their young children included, so that the early Church must have been aware of this practice [84]. Perhaps it is significant that such a practice is nowhere condemned in Scripture.

From the above it is clear that, where the baptism of "adults" (those who have reached the age of discretion) is concerned, repentance and commitment are prerequisites — indeed, the New Testament clearly links baptism with repentance. The Church has no right to baptise any candidate who has not truly repented of their sins and committed their life to Christ. These are indications of the Holy Spirit's working in a person's life, and it is this to which believers' baptism bears witness. Should it be any different where infant baptism is concerned? Surely it is only parents who have themselves come to the place of repentance and commitment in their own lives who have any right to request baptism for their infant children, since to offer one's child for baptism is to show that one means business about promoting Christianity in one's own home. It is not only a question of whether the parents themselves have been baptised: it is a question of whether the parents have kept their own covenant obligations and show evidence of the new birth in their lives, including the readiness to acknowledge Christ as Saviour and Lord, regular attendance at worship services, and a quality of life that promotes the gospel. Only if these criteria are met is the Church in any position to proclaim with certainty, through the act of baptism, that "this child, too, is a member of the covenant community".

I came across this most challenging extract in *Presbyterian Life* many years ago (exact date unknown), and would like to share it with all who read this book.

> "We are Christian parents who were determined to bring up our children in the way of the Lord, and so we entered into a rich covenant relationship with the Lord in which 'as for me and my house, we will serve the Lord' (Josh 24:15) was our watchword. We were not under the illusion that by having our children baptised they would automatically receive salvation – they needed *of their own accord* to acknowledge Jesus as Saviour and Lord, and invite Him into all aspects of their lives. Every year, on the anniversary of each child's baptism, we have a special time of family prayer and praise and once again explain to our child the importance of this covenant we have made with God and the need

for a personal response from each member of the family. The child then receives a simple Christian book, and we again spell out the need to study the Scriptures in order to deepen our relationship with Jesus." [Acknowledgement to Rob and Bridget Langley.]

A word on the practice of confirmation. In a previous paragraph I referred to the importance of a "public confession of Christ as Saviour and Lord" on the part of parents who wish to bring their child for baptism. In most Protestant Churches such a public profession is required also of prospective communicant members, and this is equated either with believers baptism or with confirmation (in those Churches in which infant baptism is practiced).

There is, in fact, no Biblical precedent for the practice of confirmation: it fulfils a utilitarian function in that it provides an opportunity for the instruction of prospective communicant members, and gives candidates an opportunity to affirm their own faith in Christ in the presence of the congregation. Thus it corresponds to one aspect of believers' baptism – public profession of faith on the part of the candidate himself – which is, by its very nature, absent from infant baptism. As such, one would expect the criteria for admission to the rite of confirmation to be equivalent to those for admission to believers' baptism. But is this the case in those Churches that make use of confirmation? Sadly, the answer in many instances has to be a resounding "no".

It was stated above that a clear profession of personal faith in the Saviour, involving both repentance and commitment, is the prerequisite for believers' baptism; now we need to affirm that this same criterion should be applied to all who wish to be confirmed. This is part of the Church's right to exercise a caring discipline over its members, and will facilitate her calling to be holy. Too often confirmation is seen as an individual's "right" when he/she reaches a pre-determined age, irrespective of whether or not they show evidence of being born again. It thus simply becomes an automatic "rite of passage" to full communicant membership of the Church.

One cause of the huge problem of "nominal membership" within to-day's Church is this virtually automatic entry into communicant membership. But there seems to me to be an additional, subsidiary reason, and that is the way in which the word "confirmation" is usually used. We speak of someone "being confirmed", implying that it is an action performed by the Church on a largely passive candidate. But surely the basic idea should be that it is the <u>candidates themselves</u> who do the confirming: that they are being given the opportunity to confirm and confess their personal faith in, and commitment to, Christ, so that the Church may rejoice with them over the Holy Spirit's saving work in their lives? And this should surely involve more than answering "yes" to a few questions put to the candidate during the confirmation service, even after a period of instruction!

As I see it, then, there are three special groups of people of whom the Church has the right to expect a believable profession of faith: those who present themselves for believers' baptism, parents who bring their young children for baptism, and those who, having been baptised as infants, wish to "be" confirmed. Would that the Church would tighten up her approach in each of these instances (even if it means saying 'no' to some prospective candidates) so that it would again be a privilege to confess Christ as Saviour and Lord rather than, as baptism-followed-by-confirmation seems to be for so many, an automatic entry into nowhere land and an uncertain hope for eternity.

1. O Father God, our children hold
    In your strong arms of love;
   Surround them, as their years unfold,
    With mercies from above.

2. We know not what the years may bring
    Of peacefulness or pain;
   Protect them when they feel life's sting,
    And keep them from sin's stain.

3. In childhood days keep them from harm,
    In youth give courage pure;
   In adulthood make strong their arm,
    In age give comfort sure.

4. Cause faith within their hearts to grow,
    Let love their spirits drive;
   Give them unfailing hope to know,
    Keep joy in them alive.

5. The cross of Christ help them to bear,
    The way of peace to show,
   That lives which they with others share,
    His heavenly life may know.

R M Samson

Chapter 14 : THE LORD'S SUPPER

Sacraments. The Lord's Supper or Holy Communion is the second of the two sacraments recognised by all branches of the Christian Church, and one of the only two recognised by the majority of Protestant Churches. It has become fashionable in modern religious *parlance* to use the terms *sacrament* or *sacramental* in a variety of contexts; thus we have, for example, statements such as "life is a sacrament", "the sacramental nature of the earth (or nature)" and, in some theological writings, the description of Christ as "God's primary Sacrament", etc. This can only lead to confusion, and it is therefore necessary at the start of this chapter to reiterate what is meant by the term here. *A sacrament is a holy ordinance or sign, instituted by Christ, which, by means of tangible and visible elements, represents and confirms the promise of the Gospel to us, namely, that because of the one sacrifice of Christ, God graciously grants forgiveness of sins and everlasting life to all believers.* Thus the sacraments are signs: they represent spiritual truths in the form of "action pictures". They also confirm and strengthen faith as, through the working of the Holy Spirit, they impact our senses and authenticate the spiritual truths that they represent.

Through the sacraments God renews His covenant promise to be our God and to grant us eternal life in Christ, but this demands a response on our part. In baptism, the candidate, or his sponsors, affirm their trust in Christ as Saviour and their intention to follow Him as Lord. In the Lord's Supper the assembled believers proclaim the sacrificial death of their Master and its faith in His return, and the members individually reaffirm their allegiance to Him.

Significance of the Lord's Supper. What is the special significance attached to the Lord's Supper? As we remember from the various New Testament passages that describe its institution by the Lord, His followers were to do it *"in remembrance of Him"*. The bread is a stark reminder of our Lord's body that was broken by the scourging and crucifixion, and the wine or grape juice is a vivid reminder of His blood that was shed for us as He died in our place and for our salvation. So whenever we meet around His Table, we are to remember Him and His death for us – His body broken and His blood shed on our behalf. And it was to be done *"until He come"*, thus reminding us that our Saviour will return again in power and great glory. So the Lord's Supper is an emphatic reminder of God's love for us and by partaking we, in turn, affirm our faith in Him. Jesus declared that the cup represented His blood of the new covenant, the covenant that has been ratified in His blood, so reminding us of all the covenant blessings that are ours in and through Christ, and that we have been called by God to be His own special people.   By the symbolism of the Supper we proclaim the wonder of the Lord's death to all who will hear.

In sharing bread from the same loaf we are reminded of our unity in Christ and that together we form part of the body of Christ; when we celebrate the Lord's Supper, we share in mutual fellowship with other believers. We are also reminded that this rite has continued down through the centuries and is being celebrated in many different countries, and so we are again made aware of our participation in the universal Church that spans both distance and time.

When we consider the other New Testament references to the Lord's Supper, we note that it is an ordinance that must be treated with the greatest respect: we are warned not to eat or drink unworthily, and are urged to examine ourselves before partaking lest we eat and drink judgement upon ourselves (1Cor 11:29). This does not mean that we cannot partake if we are aware of our sinful state – we are, after all, sinners saved by grace, and coming to the Lord's Table gives us another opportunity to confess our sinfulness – but it <u>does</u> mean that we must come as believers who seek to deepen their commitment, and that we are not harbouring any hatred or bitterness in our hearts towards other members of Christ's body. In fact, having warned the Corinthian Christians to examine themselves (1 Cor 11:28), Paul tells them (and us) that when we partake of the Lord's Supper, we must do so as *"recognising the body of the Lord"*. This *could* mean that we must remember that the elements symbolise the body of Christ sacrificed for us on the cross, but the more likely interpretation, in the light of the context and of the behaviour of the Corinthian Christians, is that we have to be aware of the communal nature of the Table and that we share in it together as the body of believers, where division (vs 18), and selfish actions and selfish behaviour (vss 20 – 22) have no place. The Corinthians' attitude led to God's judgement falling upon them in the form of physical illness and, in some cases, even death (vs 30). God forbid that this should be true of us!

"This is my body ... this is my blood". We are all aware of the visible elements of the Lord's Supper: the bread that is broken and eaten, and the wine that is poured out and shared out among those present . But these were intended to be commemorative emblems -- to commemorate His death so that we might remember Him more clearly – and the words "This is my body" and "This is my blood" were meant metaphorically, meaning no more than that the elements signify or represent His body and His blood. For one thing, Jews were forbidden to drink blood or to eat meat with the blood still in it. This prohibition was passed on to the early Christians when the apostles met to discuss the evangelistic work of Barnabas and Paul, in the following terms: *"We should write to the believers, telling them to abstain from the meat of strangled animals and from blood"* (Acts 15:20). For another, Jesus was physically present, reclining at the table with the disciples; it surely never entered their heads that He meant to say He was holding His own body and His own blood in His hands! He evidently meant, "This bread in my hand is a symbol of my body, and the wine in this cup that I hold is the symbol of my blood". Early rabbinic tradition taught that the wine represented the blood of the Passover lamb. So when Jesus lifted the third *seder* cup after the meal saying "this is my blood of the new covenant", He identified Himself as the Passover Lamb, the Messiah [85], and the wine in the cup now represented *His* blood that was to be poured out in death. In this way Jesus indicated to His disciples "that the original meaning of the Paschal rite had now been transcended" in that He is the true Paschal Lamb fulfilling the Old Testament prefigurement (1 Cor 5:7) [86].

In the light of what has been written above, I am very concerned that, during the Communion service in so many Churches, the presiding minister raises the bread (or cup) and says to the congregation "This is the body (blood) of Christ" or "The body (blood) of Christ that is broken (shed) for you". I cannot help feeling that this detracts from Christ's *real* body that was broken for me on the cross, and His *real* blood that was poured out in the agony of death for me, and I find that this introduces a jarring note into the service. I am concerned, too, that this gesture, with its accompanying words, can very easily be misunderstood or misinterpreted, especially (but not only) if children are present at the service, either as spectators or as participants (see below). Reformed doctrine is very clear that the elements are not, nor do they in any way become or contain, the body or the blood of Christ, but simply *represent* them, as the following quotation shows: *"Especially should every conception of bodily presence be suppressed. For while the elements are here in the world, seen by the eyes and felt by the hands, Christ, in so far as He is man, we must contemplate as in no place but heaven, and seek Him in no other way than with faith's understanding.*

Wherefore it is a preposterous and impious superstition to enclose Him in or under the elements of this world" [87]. To use phrases such as "this is the blood of Christ" and "the body of Christ for you", or similar, creates the impression that "something happens" to the bread and wine during the Communion service. Why not simply say what we really mean and believe?

In this connection, there is a further verse that requires our attention, namely 1 Cor 10:16: *"Is not the cup of thanksgiving for which we give thanks a participation (sharing) in the blood of Christ? And is not the bread that we break a participation (sharing) in the body of Christ?'* The basic context here (verses 14 – 22) is whether or not believers should participate in idol feasts. Paul points to the inconsistency of believers who share in the Lord's Table but also take part in the table of idols. How can they, who have shared fellowship with the Lord at His Table, and who claim to have participated in the blessings of Christ's death by partaking of the Lord's Supper, now go and drink also from the cup of demons? Eating and drinking at the Lord's Table declares our allegiance to the crucified Christ; similarly, those who participate in feasts dedicated to idols drink from the "cup of demons"; they declare their allegiance to idols and in this way become ensnared by the demonic world.

What shall we say, then, about the presence of the Lord at His Table? This is a subject that has caused controversy and division down through the centuries, and was a source of major disagreement between the reformers Calvin and Zwingli. We have already seen that, in reformed theology, the elements are not changed into the body and blood of Christ, nor is He considered to be present "in" "with" or "under" the elements of bread and wine. But as the bread and wine symbolise the body and blood of Christ, so it is suggested [88] "that Christ is also *spiritually present* as we partake of these elements". How is this to be understood? The New Testament presents three situations in which Christ promises to be present: He is present with the individual believer (e.g. John 14:23), He is present with all who go in His name as missionaries or evangelists (Matt 28:20), and He is present whenever even two or three meet together in His name (Matt 18:20). I note that no specific promise of His presence is given with respect to the Lord's Supper, where the emphasis is on remembering Him – but is such a promise needed? After all, at Communion we meet together in the His name, and so He *is* with us, and we can accept His presence in faith. But this implies that the Lord's presence with us around His Table is of the same order as His presence at a Church Bible study group or at the regular service of worship. This is not to belittle the Lord's Supper; rather, it is to rejoice that Christ is with us -- even if invisibly and "spiritually" -- *whenever* we meet together as a group of His people, however small or large the group may be. To be sure, at the Lord's Supper we have a vivid reminder of His presence with us and of His love for us, but it is that same presence which He manifests with the "two or three" meeting in His name.

"Feed on Him in your hearts by faith". This, or some similar exhortation, is included in the communion liturgies of most denominations. The wording derives, presumably, from two sources, namely from the fact that the Lord's Supper is a symbolic meal in which the bread and the cup represent Christ's body and blood, and from the discourse recorded in John 6:35-58 where Jesus several times refers to "eating My flesh and drinking My blood".

What does this somewhat strange phraseology mean – incidentally, phraseology that would have been totally abhorrent to our Lord's Jewish hearers (see John 6: 41, 52, 60)? If the passage in John 6 is allowed to be its own interpreter, we find, as has already been hinted at in chapter 12, that "eating my flesh and drinking my blood" (verse 54) is exactly parallel to "looking to the Son and believing in Him" (verse 40), and "If anyone eats of this bread (which) is my flesh" (verse 51) is exactly parallel to "he who believes" (verse 47). A notable Jewish Christian writer [89] tells us that "eating and drinking" here means "living and abiding" in Christ, and Tasker [90] comments as follows, "Jesus has come down from heaven to give His flesh offered in sacrifice, and unless men (*sic*) eat this bread, i.e. unless they accept that sacrifice in faith, they have no life in themselves". I am in full agreement with the late Bishop J. C. Ryle that these words about "eating and drinking" in John 6 were not spoken with any direct reference to the sacrament of the Lord's Supper [91], but both it and they point to the same awesome event, namely, to the atoning sacrifice of Christ through which alone we receive Life, and hence to the call to faith, commitment and allegiance to Him, our living Lord.

This is also the interpretation that seems best to suit those words in the communion liturgy, namely to "feed on Him in your heart by faith, with thanksgiving". Here, too, the reference is to a personal faith in Jesus and commitment to Him or, to paraphrase Bruce [92], "eating the flesh and drinking the blood" of Christ consists in faithfully remembering His death, believing that He has shed His blood for me, and trusting Him as my Saviour for forgiveness and cleansing from sin's stain. I am aware that many like to think of their participation at Communion as such a spiritual feeding on Christ; for my part, however, I have always found this phraseology difficult, even somewhat distasteful. I prefer to think that I am partaking *with* the Lord at His Table, as did the disciples at that first Lord's Supper on that fateful betrayal night, and also partaking with other believers in joyful thanksgiving, rather than that I am partaking *of* the Lord, even if only in a "spiritual" sense. Yet for all of us our participation at the table is, or should be, an oft-to-be-repeated practical affirmation that we are committed to Christ and seeking to live and abide in Him. But please, oh please, let it be a glad, not a sombre, celebration: let us remember our Saviour with joy and rejoice in the wonder of His love as we share in fellowship one with another, just as those early disciples "broke bread in their homes and ate together with glad and sincere hearts" (Acts 2: 46).

A Means of Grace. As with baptism, so with the Lord's Supper: obedience brings blessing! Jesus urged us to keep this ordinance as a memorial of His death, until He should come again, and our obedience in doing so will bring down His blessings upon us. As we have seen, appropriate observance of the Supper implies faith, trust and commitment on the part of those who partake. So we bring to the Table our faith and our trust in the Lord, and our commitment to Him, and as we partake, so our faith, our trust and our commitment are strengthened and deepened, and the promises of God to all believers are affirmed. At the same time we are reminded again of our Saviour's great love for us – that love which did not shrink even from death on the cross. So, as we share the Table with the Lord, and in concert with our fellow believers, rejoicing that He will come again, let our thankful hearts echo again the hymn-writer's sentiments:

> "*Amazing love, how can it be,*
> *That Thou my God shouldst die for me?*"

In this sense the Lord's Supper is rightly called "a means of grace". But let us be quite clear that no automatic or "magical" benefit comes to us from partaking of the Lord's Supper, nor does it bring salvation -- it is meant to strengthen the faith, to deepen the commitment, and to advance the mutual fellowship, of those who already know the Lord. Perhaps it is because of some of the above misapprehensions concerning the Lord's Supper that a theologian of a previous century wrote, "*The sacraments have no power to give or confer grace to the receiver, neither are they instruments of our justification, (but) they are means to confirm our faith in the promises of God. As the Spirit of God works through them, so our senses are moved and quickened by the visible elements, and our faith strengthened"* [93].

Children and the Lord's Supper. It seems appropriate at this point to say something about the place of children in the Communion service. This is a matter that has been vigorously debated over the years, and some denominations and many local Churches are still discussing this issue.

If children from Christian homes who have been baptised as infants are accepted as members of the covenant community and as members of the visible Church (chapter 12), is there any overriding reason to deny them access to the Lord's Table? I am assuming, of course, that the children are old enough and mature enough to have a basic understanding of the Lord's Supper, and that they have put their own personal trust in Jesus as Saviour. Many children have made a definite Christian commitment, and do have a basic understanding both of the gospel and of the Communion service – and the Lord will welcome them, for of such is the kingdom of heaven! After all, children within Israelite families partook of the Passover meal and its preparation, and were (and still are!) encouraged to understand the significance of that Old Testament "sacrament" by asking the question, "What does this ceremony mean to you?" (Ex 12:3,26; 13:8).

Kuyper [94] has some stern words to say about Churches that treat covenant youth as no different from pagan youth. He writes, "Comparatively few Protestant Churches take the membership of baptised children seriously. That is one reason why so few Churches today have any hold on the children of the covenant. Many Protestant Churches put their children in the same category as the children of unbelievers and pagans. If the Church does not act as though they are members, how can they be expected to think of themselves as members? Having no sense of belonging to the Church, they drift away. And if the Church regards them as heathen, small wonder if they behave like heathen." In much the same vein, a former student wrote to his professor as follows [95], "the great reason for our trouble with 'youth' is that we have systematically starved them of the Means of Grace". You might recall my plea (chapter 13) that the Church should both recognise, and take seriously, her responsibility *vis-à-vis* the children of its members.

However, there are a few matters that concern me in connection with admitting children to Communion. In the first place, as I have already intimated, the practice would have to be carefully controlled to ensure that only children who had made a believable Christian commitment, and who had some degree of understanding of the meaning of Communion, should be allowed to participate fully – other children attending the service could be invited to come forward to be blessed by the minister or by one of the Church elders. The second matter that concerns me is the ambiguous language that is normally used in our Communion liturgies. I have already expressed my concern on this matter earlier in this chapter, but it needs particular emphasis when children are allowed to participate so that they are not given wrong ideas and ultimately caused to stumble in their faith. The Church needs to mean what it says, and to say clearly what it means!

Concluding remarks. In two books that I have read recently [96, 97] the writers make a plea for a return to the simplicity of the Lord's Supper as instituted by Christ and as celebrated with joy by the earliest disciples in each other's homes (Acts 2:42, 46), a sentiment with which I wholeheartedly agree. "What is sorely needed is a return to the simplicity of the upper room: to see the Lord setting apart the bread and the wine as tokens of His approaching death, to see the disciples recciving and eating and drinking by faith, and to hear the call to continue this in the life of the Church in memory of the Master – all this is to move in an atmosphere far removed from the philosophical speculations(that we often come across today)" [96]. Would that we could move away from the idea that the Lord's Supper is a *mystery*: there seems nothing mysterious to me about Jesus breaking the bread and inviting His disciples to share the meal with Him, and then asking them to repeat the meal as a perpetual reminder of His death – and so also of His love – until His promised return. Certainly, His death in our place is a mystery, as is His abiding presence with individual believers and with those who meet together in His name, but I do not find anything mysterious about the celebration of the Lord's Supper itself. Let us celebrate it simply and joyfully, for the sake both of our children and of ourselves.

Following on from this, let us not overstate the importance of the Lord's Supper. Of course it is important in the communal life of believers, but so is the faithful preaching and exposition of God's word, so is corporate prayer, and so are the worship, praise and adoration brought by God's people when they meet together in His presence. I note that of all the New Testament letters, the Lord's Supper is mentioned in only one (namely 1 Corinthians). As the late Bishop Ryle wrote, "The Lord's Supper is not in its right place when it is made the first and most important thing in Christian worship. We may well ask, 'What warrant of Scripture is there for this extravagant honour?'". And elsewhere [98] he points out that "to repent and be converted, to believe and to be holy, to be born again and have grace in our hearts – all these things are of far more importance than to be a communicant. Without them we cannot be saved; without the Lord's Supper we can. Are you tempted to make the Lord's Supper override and overshadow everything else in Christianity and to place it above prayer and preaching? Take care; mind what you are about!".

In this connection, let us also take note of the implied warning in Heb 13:9: "*It is good for our hearts to be strengthened by grace, not by ceremonial foods*". The primary reference here is to the teaching of those Judaizers who insisted that participation in certain Jewish ritual meals was essential for salvation. But let us not fall into their error of emphasizing the external ritual of eating and drinking at the Lord's Table to such an extent that reliance solely on God's grace is pushed into the background. For this reason, I am concerned that so many believers look upon the Lord's supper as their "spiritual food" for the coming week or month. Surely our spiritual food comes from our close walk with the Lord day-by-day, our study and meditation on His word, and time spent in prayer and worship?

I wish to close this chapter with some practical observations. The first is this: I can find no scriptural reason for insisting, as some denominations do, that only an ordained minister may officiate at the Lord's Table. Certainly, a communion service must be conducted with reverence and decorum or, as the Bible says in a slightly different context, "in a fitting and orderly way" (1 Cor 14:40). But there are many lay leaders who are perfectly competent and could be trusted to conduct a Communion service in a most acceptable manner. This would certainly take pressure off some ministers, particularly in rural areas, who travel frequently, and often over vast distances, to serve Communion to outlying congregations. But my point here is not so much one of expediency as of principle.

Then there is the bread that is broken: would it not be more fitting to use an actual loaf of bread that is broken in full view of the congregation, rather than little pre-cut cubes as happens in so many Churches? I remember the forceful impression made on me the first time I saw an actual loaf of bread being broken during a Communion service. And why not invite two elders or lay members, in place of the minister, to give thanks for the bread and for the cup at appropriate places in the service, so giving lay members of the congregation a greater part in our celebration around the Lord's Table?

The final point I make is this: why does the Communion liturgy of so many denominations stipulate that the officient, usually the minister, and his/her assistants should serve themselves <u>first</u>? This seems contrary both to good manners on the part of the acting host(!), as well as contrary to our Lord's own teaching on servant-hood and the first being last, etc. Our Lord, at the institution of His Supper, broke bread and then gave it to the disciples, and similarly with the cup (Matt 26:26, 27), without partaking first Himself.

1. Our Master's love remember,
   Exceeding great and free;
   Lift up thy heart in gladness,
   For He remembers thee.

2. Bring every weary burden,
   Thy sin, thy fear, thy grief;
   He calls the heavy-laden,
   And gives them kind relief.

3. Sit down beneath His shadow,
   And rest with great delight;
   The faith that now beholds Him
   Is pledge of future sight.

4. A little while, though parted --
   Remember, wait, and love,
   Until He comes in glory,
   Until we meet above.

5. Till in the Father's kingdom
   The heavenly feast is spread,
   And we behold His beauty,
   Whose blood for us was shed.

Frances Ridley Havergal
(Order of verses changed.)

Chapter 15 : "THAT OLD SERPENT, THE DEVIL"

Is there such a being as the devil? There are some who deny his existence, and suggest that, where the devil or Satan is mentioned in Scripture, this represents simply a personification of evil [99]. Similarly, demons are dismissed as the fanciful creation of the pagan mind [100a], and the instances of demon possession recorded in the Bible are said to be straightforward cases of epilepsy or other known medical conditions [100b]. And we are told that, when Jesus spoke about demons "He was simply accommodating His speech to fit in with the common ideas prevalent at the time." What shall we say in response to such teaching? *

In response, the first point to note is that Satan is described as "the father of lies" (John 8:44), and nothing would please him more than that people should believe his greatest lie, namely, that neither he nor his demons have any real existence. The second important point is that, if Jesus came to bear witness to the truth [John 1:14, 17;3:11; 8:44-46 (said in connection with the devil) and John 14:6], He would not have propagated error in order to fit in with contemporary ideas. Instead, He constantly pointed out error whenever and wherever He encountered it. Then, in Rev 20:2, we read about *"the dragon, that ancient serpent, who is the devil, or Satan"*; here *the dragon* and *ancient serpent* are clearly figurative terms, whereas *the devil, or Satan* is the reality behind the figures. There is no suggestion that these terms refer only to a "personification of evil".

The devil : his power and influence. We must attempt to put this whole matter into perspective. The New Testament warns us to be on our guard against the devil and his wily schemes (Eph 6:11). Our ultimate battle – whether in terms of our own daily living as Christians, or whether in terms of our efforts to spread the gospel so that others may come to salvation – is not against material forces, but *against the powers of this dark world and against spiritual forces of evil in the heavenly realms* (Eph 6:12). This does not mean that every time we sin we can clear our consciences by blaming this unseen enemy: we ourselves are responsible for our own sins and failures. Nor does it mean

---

* *Systematic Theology* by Wayne Grudem is most helpful on the Scriptural teaching regarding the devil and demons, and I acknowledge my debt to this work for material included in this chapter. Another most useful book on the subject of demons is *Like a Roaring Lion* by Robert & Martha Peterson [101].

that there is a demon behind every bush or under every stone! But it does mean that there are evil forces that oppose God's will and plan, that their influence is to be met with spiritual resources, and that we need to be aware of our enemy's cunning and strength. So we have to be strong *in the Lord and in His mighty power* (Eph 6:10). A very real, even if spiritual, battle is in progress, and God seeks our involvement in the fight against the evil one and his minions. For this reason we need to know something of our enemy and his stratagems.

The Bible leaves us in no doubt as to the existence of Satan and his servants, the demons. But it also shows us quite clearly that Satan's activities are, ultimately, under God's control – the devil is not a divine being like God, and his power and influence are limited by the constraints that God places upon him.

In addition, he is already a defeated foe. Jesus defeated him by His death on the cross and through His mighty resurrection; thus the devil's fate is sealed. But do not underestimate the power and fury of the devil in this, his death agony! In fact, the fullness of his anger has yet to be vented against the inhabitants of the earth as he sees his time drawing to a close (Rev 12:12). He is described as *"prowling around like a roaring lion looking for someone to devour* (1 Pet 5:8); at other times he or his demons come to us masquerading as "angels of light" or "servants of righteousness" (2 Cor 11:14-15), endued with the power to work counterfeit miracles and "lying wonders" (2 Thes 2:9, AV) in order to deceive humankind. Jesus described the devil as "a murderer" and "a liar and the father of lies" for "there is no truth in him" (John 8:44). So Paul exhorts his readers to *"put on the full armour of God so that you can take your stand against the devil's schemes* (or *"strategies and tricks"*, NLT) (Eph 6:11).

The tragedy of all this is that the devil, "the god of this age", *"has blinded the minds of those who do not believe, and prevents the light of the glorious gospel of Christ, the image of God, from shining on them"* (2 Cor 4:4, Phillips), so that now *"the whole world is under the control of the evil one"* (1 John 5:19). Little wonder that Paul tells us that we (believers) *"have been rescued from the dominion of darkness and brought into the kingdom of God's Son"* (Col 1:13) so that we, in turn, might be used by God to rescue others and bring them to the light of Christ.

The work of Satan and his demons. We must now consider the activity of Satan in slightly greater detail. But first we must remind ourselves that Satan is not God: he is neither all-powerful nor is he omniscient. For example, he did not foresee that the cross, which seemed to be his greatest triumph, would, in fact, lead to his ultimate defeat, and that from it would flow the greatest good ever to come into the world. Nor is Satan everywhere present; for this reason, much of his nefarious work is carried out by demons, probably fallen angels who have been drawn into the service of their new master by his lies and deceits. So when we speak about Satan's activities, we also include the work of demons as well. What, then, are the various activities associated with Satan and demons?

We have already come across some of Satan's work, namely his work of deception as he disguises himself as "an angel of light" and/or as he performs miracles in order to lead people astray. We have also seen that he creates spiritual blindness so that men and women are unable to appreciate their need of salvation or to recognise Jesus as the Saviour they need. In the parable of the sower Jesus warns that Satan is able to take away God's word that has been "sown" in people's hearts (Matt 13:19); as Torrey [102] points out, "wherever the word is preached Satan is present, either in person or through his agents, to snatch away the seed sown". And where he is unable to snatch away the seed, he attempts to exert a corrupting influence by mixing the growing plants with a look-alike weed (Matt 13:24-30).* Thus Satan will use every kind of destructive activity in seeking to turn people away from God and to lead them ultimately into eternal separation from God.

That the devil is active, too, in the lives of believers is clear from Scripture. He attempts to hinder us from doing the Lord's work (1 Thes 2:18); the Lord allows him to test believers (Job 1; Luke 22:31), including stirring up persecution against them (Rev 2:10); and he is able to oppress God's people in various ways. For example, Paul was given a "thorn in the flesh, a messenger of Satan" (2 Cor 12:7) – but even this was under God's control, and was God's means of keeping Paul humble in the light of the special task that was entrusted to him. I know, too, from personal experience, that Satan is able to cause misunderstanding to arise out of remarks made in all innocence and

---

* The "weeds" to which Jesus referred in this parable would probably have been darnel, a well-known poisonous weed that looks very much like wheat when the plants are young, but can be distinguished from the wheat when the plants mature.

sincerity, and thus to stir up dissension, and even division, within the Church. Thus he uses human frailty and fallibility to further his own wicked purposes.

We know from the gospel accounts that Jesus was tempted by the devil, not only at the start of His public ministry but also at other "opportune times" (Luke 4:13). And shall <u>we</u> escape such attention from the evil one? The answer surely is "no": we, too, can and must expect demonic attack in the form of temptation, and must constantly be on our guard against it. As I have already stated, not all sin is caused by Satan or demons, and we must never blame demons for our sins and failures; nevertheless, it seems reasonable to conclude that the New Testament is telling us that there is some degree of demonic influence in most wrongdoing and sin that occurs today, including in the lives of Christians. And where there is a pattern of persistent sin in the life of a Christian, especially if the individual concerned has prayed and struggled for victory, it could be that he/she is under demonic influence relating to that situation.

Demons. Perhaps it is appropriate at this stage to say something specifically about demons, an area about which many Christians know little, and some might even treat with scepticism, even though they are conversant with the idea of a personal devil, viz., Satan.

The *origin* of the demons is shrouded in mystery. They are possibly "fallen angels" – angels who sinned and so lost their privilege of serving God and were drawn into the service of Satan, the chief of the demonic host; now they continually work evil in the world and oppose God and His kingdom at every turn. But this is largely conjecture, as Scripture does not explain the origin of demons clearly. The important thing for us is not where demons came from, but the fact, so plainly portrayed in the Bible, that demons have a real existence. What we do know is that they are created spirit beings with moral judgement and high intelligence, and that they are constantly at war against the servants of God, both angelic and human.

It is important to note that the gospel record is careful to distinguish between illness (including epilepsy) on the one hand, and demon possession on the other, even though the symptoms might be fairly similar at times (see, for example, Matt 4:24), and we would be well advised to do the same. Jesus *<u>heals</u>* the sick, but *<u>casts out</u>* demons. Although it seems unlikely that a Christian can be "demon possessed" (we are <u>God's</u> possession, and He will not normally allow joint ownership with evil powers!), as indicated above Christians may nonetheless experience demonic <u>oppression</u>, resulting in, *inter alia*, physical and psychological manifestations, including allergic reactions and depression, which cannot be brought under control by normal measures. However, it is important to realise that not all allergies or all cases of depression are the result of demonic activity! This is not the place to give a full description of signs associated with demon possession or with the whole field of deliverance ministry for those who are under demonic influence; the interested reader is referred to the excellent treatment by the Petersons [101].

In New Testament times people were very aware of demonic activity and influence in the lives of some unfortunate individuals. The same is true today in countries where the gospel has not yet penetrated very deeply: demonic activity is well known and feared, and missionaries testify both to the reality and to the widespread occurrence of such phenomena [101]. Even in our "sophisticated" western culture demonic activity, though apparently not as prevalent, is still discernable, and this includes various forms of Satan worship, spiritism and shamanism. With the steady increase in interest in the occult that we have witnessed in recent years, and its increasing exposure on television and in the written media, it is likely that demonic activity will become more noticeable in our society. And let us not fool ourselves – demons and their destructive activities are real; they are not simply the products of over-active or naïve Christian imaginations!

Our response, and our responsibility. The Bible gives us a three-fold response to Satan and his demonic activities. Firstly, we must make sure that we do not give Satan a foothold in our lives, either by giving way to anger, resentment and an unforgiving attitude (Eph 4:27), or by meddling in occult practices and activities such as fortune-telling, astrology, séances, Ouija board activities and "glassie-glassie" and, I would add, transcendental meditation. As the Christians in Corinth were warned that behind the "harmless" idolatry of pagan society there lurked a hierarchy of demons (1 Cor 10:19-20), so let us take warning that behind "innocent" flirtation with the occult that same demonic pack lies in wait. Secondly, we are told to "resist the devil, and he will flee from you" (Jas 4:7) with the implication that "*if* you resist the devil, he *will* flee from you".   How do we do this in practice? By not yielding to temptation -- we must not allow the devil to entice us into committing sin [remember our Lord's example of using the words of Scripture when He was called upon to resist the devil in the wilderness of temptation (Luke 4:1ff)] -- and by yielding ourselves more fully to God in "active allegiance" as opposed to a passive submission or apathetic resignation [**102**].

And thirdly, we are exhorted to *"be strong in the Lord and in His mighty power. Put on the full armour of God so that you can take your stand against the devil's schemes"* (Eph 6:10ff). Unaided human effort is inadequate in the spiritual battle against our powerful foe. We need both God's strength and God's armour: the belt of truth, symbolising a life of sincerity, devoid of hypocrisy, with which we can defeat Satan's lies; the breastplate of righteousness, both personal righteousness and the righteousness that comes from God through faith in Christ; footwear consisting of an understanding of and dependence on the gospel, this ("like the hobnail sandals of the Roman soldier" [**103**]) gives us a firm foundation or foothold so that we may be able to stand unmoved against the foe; faith, like the large Roman shield made of leather that could be soaked in water in order to extinguish flame-tipped arrows, which keeps us positive despite insults, setbacks and difficulties; and the helmet of salvation – the experience of Christ's saving power that both protects our minds from doubting God's saving work in our lives, and is also (as it was for the Roman soldier) a striking symbol of victory. Finally, God has given us the sword of the Spirit, His word, our only offensive weapon. With it we are enabled to overcome temptation, and by means of its message men and women are brought to the Saviour, liberated from the kingdom of Satan and added to the kingdom of God's dear Son.

But our responsibility *vis-à-vis* Satan goes further. Christians need to realise that Jesus has given <u>all</u> believers the authority to rebuke demons and to command them to leave. The work of Christ on the cross is the ultimate basis for our authority over demons – that was the event which ushered in the beginning of the end for Satan, where his final defeat was sealed. It is by faith in that victory won on the cross, and in the power of God, that we dare to rebuke the demons in Jesus' name and to exercise authority over them. Although not everyone is called to a deliverance ministry, any believer may be called upon at any time to minister to someone who is being oppressed by a demon. We could, with their permission, rebuke the demon in their presence and command it in Jesus' name to leave and never to return, or we could do this on their behalf in private when we pray for them; in either case, we will be engaging in spiritual warfare against the enemy. Notice that we <u>*rebuke*</u> and _command_ the demons with the authority of Jesus and in His name; we do not _ask_ them to leave, far less do we _pray_ to them (or to Satan) to do so.

A brief comparison of the work of the Holy Spirit with that of Satan. It is perhaps of interest, as we near the end this chapter, to compare the work of the Holy Spirit with the work of Satan. I have therefore drawn up the following brief, and doubtless incomplete, table of comparison. Note that the last few entries show that, at times, the devil attempts to mimic the Holy Spirit of God.

The Holy Spirit	The devil (including demons)
He is the Holy Spirit	He is the evil one (1 John 5:19)
He brings to remembrance the teachings of Christ (John 14:26)	He snatches away the seed that is sown in men's hearts (Luke 8:12)
He teaches us the truth about God and ourselves (1 Cor 2:12,14; John 16:8-11)	He blinds the eyes, especially of unbelievers (2 Cor 4:4)
He brings us new life (Rom 8:6)	He is a murderer and brings death (John 8:44; Heb 2:14)
He produces the fruit of the Spirit in our lives (Gal 5:22-23)	He puts wicked schemes into the minds of men (Acts 5:3)
He promotes the spread of the gospel (Acts 1:8)	He hinders the work of God and the spread of the gospel (1 Thes 2:18)
He sets people free (Rom 8:2)	He brings people into bondage (Luke 13:16)
He guides us into the truth (John 16:13)	He is a liar and the father of lies (John 8:44)
He testifies with our spirits that we are God's children (Rom 8:16)	He accuses believers before God (Rev 12:10)
He baptises and fills us (Acts 1:5; 2:4)	Demons are able to take possession of individuals (Luke 4:33)
He brings us into the kingdom of light (Acts 26:18)	He masquerades as an angel of light, but brings darkness (2 Cor 11:14)
He works miracles that display God's power (1 Cor 2:4,5)	He works miracles in order to delude humankind (2 Thes 2:9,10)

It seems that we can have either truth or lies. If we are willing to do God's will, He will lead us into His truth (John 7:17), but if we are unwilling to seek God's will, Satan will lead us step by step into apathy, delusion and error

The final destiny of Satan and his hosts. According to the Bible, *"the reason the Son of God appeared was to destroy the devil's work"* (1 John 3:8). This began on the cross (ironically, just when Satan thought that he had destroyed the Son of God) when Jesus *"made a public spectacle"* of Satan and his host *"and triumphed over them"* (Col 2:15), a triumph that was further validated by the resurrection of Jesus from the dead. So we are told that *"He (Jesus) shared in our humanity so that by death He might destroy him who holds the power of death – that is, the devil"* (Heb 2:14). As has already been mentioned, we know that the devil is a defeated foe although he and his demons are clearly still very active in the world. But we are witnessing his death throes; ultimately, the devil's influence will be totally shattered and the devil himself will be cast into the *"lake of burning sulphur and tormented day and night for ever and ever"* (Rev 20:10). This is *"the fire prepared for the devil and his angels"* to which Jesus referred in Matt 25:41; this event will signal the final overthrow of Satan and the end of all that is evil, rebellious, sinful and impure.

Personal application. I close this chapter with a brief example of how we may apply Christ's victory over Satan's host in our own lives should the need arise, taken largely from Grudem, page 430, with acknowledgements to Wayne Grudem [104]. If we discover unusually powerful sinful emotions, such as irrational fear, anger, hatred, bitterness, lust or greed, etc, welling up in our hearts and minds, in addition to asking Jesus for help in overcoming them, it could be helpful for us to say something like, "Spirit of bitterness *(for example)*, through the power of God and in the name of Jesus, I command you to leave me and never to return!" Even though we may be unsure whether there is demonic involvement or not, such words of rebuke could be highly effective in closing the door to any demonic influence in the situation. In addition, if we or one of our children wakes up with a frightening dream or recurring nightmare, as well as praying to Jesus for comfort and protection, we might also say, "In the name of Jesus, I command any evil spirit causing this frightening dream to leave and not to return!" Children from a very young age can be taught to say "In Jesus name, go away!" to any images of witches, goblins, etc that may appear in their dreams or to any other mental images that trouble them at night, and then to ask Jesus for protection and happy, comforting thoughts of Him. Such actions by little children who trust in Christ will often be remarkably effective, for their faith in Jesus is very simple and genuine (see Matt 18:1-4). But once again it must be emphasised that not all sinful motives and actions, not all errant emotions or thoughts, and not all bad dreams and nightmares, are of demonic origin. We still carry with us our sinful natures, and come across worldly enticements in our daily lives and in the media, so that our fight is against the world and the flesh, as well as against the devil. We are ultimately responsible for the way in which we live, and we need the Holy Spirit's power to help us as we strive for victory in each one of these theatres of spiritual warfare.

1. We rest on Thee, our Shield and our Defender!
    We go not forth alone against the foe;
  Strong in Thy strength, safe in Thy keeping tender,
    We rest on Thee, and in Thy name we go;
  Strong in Thy strength, safe in Thy keeping tender,
    We rest on Thee, and in Thy name we go.

2. Yes in Thy name, O Captain of salvation!
    In Thy dear name, all other names above:
  Jesus our Righteousness, our sure Foundation,
    Our Prince of glory, and our King of love;
  Jesus our Righteousness, our sure Foundation,
    Our Prince of glory, and our King of love.

3. We go in faith, our own great weakness feeling,
    And needing more each day Thy grace to know;
  Yet from our hearts a song of triumph pealing,
    We rest on Thee, and in Thy name we go;
  Yet from our hearts a song of triumph pealing,
    We rest on Thee, and in Thy name we go.

4. We rest on Thee, our Shield and our defender!
    Thine is the battle, Thine shall be the praise.
  When passing through the gates of pearly splendour,
    Victors, we rest with Thee through endless days;
  When passing through the gates of pearly splendour,
    Victors, we rest with Thee through endless days.

Edith Gilling Cherry

Chapter 16 : THE WINDING-UP OF HISTORY

On a pleasant afternoon in the late summer of 1967 I was admiring the Grand Canal in Amsterdam while standing on one of the bridges spanning the waterway, when an attractive young student approached me. She informed me that the Messiah had secretly returned to earth, that he was in hiding till the time was right for his grand appearing, and that in the mean time she was collecting money for his Cause. I should have told her (but, sadly, neglected to do so) that the coming of the True Messiah would be like lightning which, when it strikes in the east is visible even in the west (Matt 24:27) as it lights up the sky from one end to the other (Luke 17:24), and that when He came every eye would see him (Rev 1:7). Again, I should have warned her, *"Men will tell you, 'There he is, out in the desert!' or 'Here he is, in the inner rooms', but do not believe it, and do not go running off after them"* (Matt 24:26 & Luke 17:23) for many false "christs" will appear. I refused to give her any money for her Cause, and subsequently prayed that the Lord would open her eyes to recognise and to acknowledge the <u>real</u> Christ as her Saviour.

The return of Jesus Christ. There is much that we do not know or cannot understand about the second coming of Jesus, when He will return in triumph and every knee will bow before Him. The Bible teaches very clearly that He will return *in person*, that His coming will not be in secret but will be seen by all, but also that, before it happens, many rumours will circulate that Christ has returned, but in secret (as we saw above), and false christs and false prophets will perform signs and miracles, deceiving many (Mark 13:22, etc). But when it really happens, it will signal the winding-up of history as we know it, and will usher in the kingdom of God in all its glory and fullness. It will also herald the time for God's judgement of the living and of the dead.

Jesus warned us to be ready and on our guard because His coming would be both unexpected and sudden, and even He Himself did not know when it would happen. At the same time, He gave us signs that would precede His coming (Matt 24), most of which have probably not yet been fulfilled.* These

---

* Following Grudem [105], I have purposely been vague at this point since we cannot know for certain whether or not, in God's eyes, these signs have or have not yet been fulfilled. The door is thus left open for a possible imminent return of Christ, but credence is still given to the possibility that some/all of these signs still await a final fulfilment before the **[continued on page 120.]**

signs include a time of serious and violent persecution of believers, a turning away from the Christian faith, with the love of many for Jesus growing cold, the gospel being preached in the whole world, and signs appearing in the heavens involving the sun, moon and stars before *"the coming of the great and dreadful day of the Lord "* (Joel 2:31). There are also prophecies which seem to suggest that a decisive battle will occur, possibly in the Middle East, as a prelude to the Second Coming (Dan 11:36-45; Rev 16:13-16).

I am not in a position to put these events in order, or to comment on the nature or timing of the *millennium* (Rev 20:1-6) and its sequel (Rev 20:7-10). I am content to leave all of this in God's hands, for Him to arrange as He sees fit. I tend to have a healthy disregard for predictions concerning the date of the Lord's return, because they will almost certainly be wrong, as has been proved so often in the past, and I am even uncomfortable when I hear suggestions that it will take place "soon" or that "His coming is near", because I have heard it all before! We have been told so clearly that we do not and cannot know when it will occur, and false predictions simply bring the gospel into disrepute. My focus has rather been on the <u>*fact*</u> of His coming, and on the Biblical warnings, impressive in their number, that we must be ready <u>at all times</u> to welcome Him back <u>at any time</u>. As Peter wrote (2 Pet 3:12, Phillips), believers should live as people who are *"expecting, and earnestly longing for, the coming of the day of God"*, and John closes his *Revelation* with the words, *"Even so, come, Lord Jesus"* (Rev 22:20). Have you ever expressed a longing such as this for the return of the Saviour?

We have been warned! It is surprising to discover how many warnings are given to believers to be ready for the Lord's return. This theme permeates much of our Lord's teaching both in His discourses and in His parables, and the New Testament letters also contain a number of exhortations to be ready for His return. Perhaps it would be helpful, as well as challenging, to list a selection of these exhortations and then to consider some of their implications. Please take the time to read this "catalogue" of Scripture references and let them speak to your heart and mind!

> <u>Matt 24:37, 40</u>. *As it was in the days of Noah, so it will be at the coming of the Son of Man....Two men will be in the field; one will be taken and the other left*

[Continued from page 119.] Second Coming takes place. Some of these signs, as for example the persecution of believers, have been in the process of being fulfilled since the first century AD!

Matt 24: 42, 44. *Therefore keep watch, because you do not know on what day your Lord will come ...So you also must be ready, because the Son of Man will come at an hour when you do not expect Him. Also 24: 46,50 and Matt 25:13.*

Mark 13: 32 - 33, 36 - 37. *No one knows about that day or hour, not even the angels in heaven, nor the Son, but only the Father. Be on guard! Be alert! You do not know when that time will come. If He comes suddenly, do not let Him find you sleeping. What I say to you, I say to everyone: Watch!*

Luke 12: 35 - 36, 40. *Be dressed ready for service and keep your lamps burning, like men waiting for their master to return ... You also must be ready, for the Son of Man is coming at an unexpected hour.*

Luke 21:34 - 35. *Be careful, or your hearts will be weighed down with dissipation, drunkenness and the anxieties of life, and that day will close on you unexpectedly, like a trap.*

Phil 3:20. *But our citizenship is in heaven. And we eagerly await a Saviour from there, the Lord Jesus Christ.*

1 Thes 5:2,4. *You know very well that the day of the Lord will come like a thief in the night ... But you, brothers, are not in darkness so that this day should surprise you like a thief.*

Titus 2:12-13. *(God's grace) teaches us to ... live self-controlled, upright and godly lives in this present age, while we wait for the blessed hope, the glorious appearing of our great God and Saviour Jesus Christ.*

Heb 10:25. *Let us encourage one another, and all the more as you see the Day approaching.*

James 5:7. *Be patient and stand firm, the Lord's coming is near.*

Rev 22:7, 12, 20. *Behold, I am coming soon. Yes, I am coming soon. Amen; come, Lord Jesus.*

The Bible draws a number of lessons from this teaching on the unexpectedness and unpredictability of the Lord's second coming. The first (and obvious) is that we need to be ready for His coming so that we do not leave it too late, lest He were to close the door on us and say "sorry, I never knew you" (Matt 25:10-12). If you intend to commit your life to Jesus Christ as your Lord and Saviour "one day", **do it now, whatever the cost,** so that you will not find yourself excluded on that day when the last trumpet sounds and the elect are gathered in from all corners of the earth. (Matt 24:31). Furthermore, Jesus urges us to *"watch"* (Mark 13:37, etc), that is, to expect the unexpected and to be ready for it, and to be on our guard that Satan does not cause us to stumble as we wait for Jesus to return.

The second important implication of Christ's sudden return is that His people, the believers, should be living such transparent lives that they will not be ashamed of their lifestyle if the Lord were to arrive unexpectedly. John tells us, *"When He appears, we shall be like Him, (and) everyone who has this hope in Christ purifies himself, just as He is pure"* (1 John 3:3). As Grudem puts it, "I frequently examine my heart and my life to see if there is anything of which I would be ashamed when Jesus returns, because I want to be ready for Him to return at any moment, even at a moment I do not expect" **[105]**. And Paul emphasises this point when he writes: *(God's grace) teaches us to ... live self-controlled, upright and godly lives in this present age, while we wait for the blessed hope, the glorious appearing of our great God and Saviour, Jesus Christ* (Titus 2:12-13). This implies, as well, that we should continue to do our daily work to the best of our ability, even if we do think that Christ's coming is just around the corner! Then there is the work of evangelism: Jesus spoke about the coming of "night" when no more work would be possible (John 9:4); therefore let us labour to bring others to Jesus while we still have the opportunity to do so – while it is still "day".

Finally, belief in the second coming of Jesus, unpredictable as its timing is, should serve to encourage us, not only to do our best for Him in respect of life and witness while we await His return, but also to encourage one another with the fact that the Lord is coming – and it could be soon! (1 Thes 4:17,18). And Jesus encourages us to *"stand up, and lift up your heads, because your redemption is drawing near"* when we see the signs beginning to be fulfilled (Luke 21:28).

<u>**"I am coming soon"-- was Jesus mistaken?**</u> This quotation, taken from Rev 22:7, tells us that Jesus would return to the earth "soon". But nearly two thousand years have elapsed, and still the world awaits His coming. Does this mean that both Jesus and the writers of the New Testament were wrong in their expectation that the second coming would happen "soon"? What does

the New Testament mean by "soon" in this context?

In the first place, we are reminded in the Bible that God, "who inhabits eternity", does not "see" time as we do, so that "soon" in His vocabulary might not have the same meaning as "soon" in ours. Thus Peter writes, *"... with the Lord one day is as a thousand years, and a thousand years as one day"* (2 Pet 3:8). Then, too, the Bible is clear that God is patiently waiting, giving more people the opportunity to be saved before the door to the kingdom is finally closed: *"The Lord is not slow in keeping His promise as some understand slowness; He is patient with you, not wanting anyone to perish, but everyone to come to repentance"* (2 Pet 3:9).

Furthermore, scholars have long been aware that Biblical prophecy is not normally concerned with details of chronology: future events are seen in what may be described as a two-dimensional outline which does not include the intervening time before, or between, the events that are to take place. One result of this is that "the future was always viewed as imminent ... the (Biblical) prophets blended the near and distant perspectives so as to form a single canvas" **[106]**.

Finally, we noted in a previous paragraph that we should encourage one another, and ourselves too, with the knowledge that Jesus is coming again, and that it might be "any day now". But what kind of encouragement would it have been to the early Christians, just when they needed it most, to be told that Jesus would return in two (or five-) thousand years' time? And what motivation would this have provided for sober and holy living, and for faithfulness in completing the work to which the Lord had called them? The answer, clearly, is none at all! Although Jesus, by His own admission, did not know the date of His return, He was presumably aware of the task that lay ahead for His people and that this would take many centuries or even millennia to complete. He knew that we needed the constant encouragement and motivation of His promised coming again, as well as the reminder of our allegiance to Him through our regular attendance at His Table, as we – the Church – face the daunting tasks of spreading the gospel throughout the world and of living as shining lights *"in a crooked and depraved generation"* (Phil 3:15). Even so, come Lord Jesus -- come as King to reign!

The final act in the drama. The second coming of Jesus will signal the final act in the drama of salvation, and the Scriptures suggest that the following occurrences might be associated with His return, possibly in the order indicated:

- a time of intense persecution of Christians;
- a period of unprecedented hardship and tribulation on earth ("the great tribulation"), allowed by God in His mercy as a last call to men and women everywhere to turn to Him in repentance, during which time, too, many Jews will recognise Jesus as their Messiah and Saviour;
- the return of Jesus to reign as King, linked with the resurrection of those who died "in Christ" and who will rise to meet Him "in the air";
- **possibly** a prolonged period of peace and righteousness (the *millennium*, which could also happen *before* the Lord's return, or it might not be a period of time on earth at all, depending on how one interprets Scripture);
- a final revolt against God, instigated by Satan, which will lead to the Battle of Armageddon and the ultimate victory of Christ over Satan,
- to be followed by the resurrection of the rest of humankind, the final judgement, and the coming of the new heavens and the new earth.

All of this is suggested or hinted at in Scripture, but the order in which the events will occur is not without controversy as this subject lends itself to various different interpretations: the details are not always clear, and (for example) at least three different approaches regarding the *millennium* are possible, as was suggested above, depending on how the text is interpreted. That said, there is no ambiguity concerning the major truths set forth: the return of Jesus, the ultimate defeat of Satan, and the final separation of humankind before God's judgement throne. It is this last truth that we now need to consider, difficult and sombre as it may be.

That such a final separation is foretold in the Bible no one can deny. Several of our Lord's parables speak of such a separation, and the remainder of the New Testament refers to this theme again and again, either directly or by implication. To give some examples from the mouth of the Lord Himself:

Matt 13:30. *"At that time I will tell the harvesters: 'First collect the weeds and tie them in bundles to be burned; then gather the wheat and bring it into my barn'."*

Matt 25:41,46. *"Then He will say to those on His left, 'Depart from me, you who are cursed, into the eternal fire prepared for the devil and his angels.'...Then they will go away to eternal punishment, but the righteous to eternal life."*

Luke17:30, 35. *"It will be just like this on the day the Son of Man is revealed....Two women will be grinding grain together; one will be taken and the other left".*

In Rev 20:12-15 we are given a vivid description of the final judgement. The resurrected dead -- both great and small, believers and non-believers alike; none were excepted – stood before the throne of God as *"the books were opened."* These books evidently contained a record of the deeds of all human beings, and the dead were judged according to what they had done as recorded in these books. But there was another book that was also opened, mentioned separately and thus, it seems, of special importance, called the *Book of Life* (Rev 20:12,15) and *the Lamb's Book of Life* (Rev 21:27). This book is also of sombre significance, for we read, *"If anyone's name was not found written in the Book of Life, he was thrown into the lake of fire"*, echoing the words of Jesus quoted above: *'Depart from me, you who are cursed, into the eternal fire prepared for the devil and his angels'* (Matt 25:46).

Perhaps it would be appropriate to pause for a moment's reflection. We are now considering teaching that, for many people (myself included) is highly unpalatable -- the wrath of God, the lake of fire, eternal separation from God, etc. I wish I could write it differently, perhaps that all will eventually be saved or, at worst, that God's judgement of the wicked will lead to their complete annihilation rather than their being cast into hell (i.e., the lake of fire which is "the second death" [*]). But the Biblical testimony does not permit of such an approach, and I have no authority for making the clear teaching of the Bible more palatable to human sensibilities. I would far rather warn people of God's coming judgement and in the end find that I was wrong, than to expound a gospel of "salvation for all, irrespective" and **then** find that I had been wrong in not warning the careless and indifferent!

---

[*] The terms *death* and *destruction* in these contexts do not imply the cessation of existence, but speak of exclusion from the Lord's presence, and of the harmful effects and the devastation produced by the final judgement, namely the ruin of life and all its proud accomplishments [107].

Of particular relevance here, of course, is the teaching of Jesus Himself – He who came from the Father, declared that He knew the Father's mind and will, and emphasised that what He taught was the truth. He has left us in no doubt about the awful reality of hell: He was careful to warn men and women to repent from their wickedness, to turn to Him in faith, and to ensure that they entered through the "narrow gate" that leads to life, rather than through the "wide gate" that leads to destruction * (Matt 7:13-14). And in His teaching He frequently referred to "weeping and gnashing of teeth" in order to underscore the seriousness of what He was saying. What we can and must affirm is that God's judgements are fair and righteous (Rev 16:7 and 19:2). "We need not fear that justice will not be done: it will! But precisely because of that sinners must tremble" before a righteous and loving God **[108]**. There is no escaping from the consequences of one's sin – the books will be opened, and all will be revealed.

The thoughtful reader will have noticed that, although judgement is based on what each person had done in this life, their final destiny depends on whether their names are written in the *Book of Life* or not. We are not saved by our deeds** – good deeds cannot atone for sin, and anyway we all fall far short of God's requirements -- but deeds do provide clear evidence of a person's actual relationship with God in Jesus Christ and, therefore, whether their name will be found written in the Book of Life. The New Testament often states that judgement is on the basis of our deeds, but that salvation itself depends on personal trust in Jesus. And the fact that God does take our deeds into account in pronouncing His judgements means that His judgements will be fair and righteous, as is emphasised in Rev 16:5 & 7, and 19:2. For believers, the wonderful truth on the day of judgement will be that *"there is therefore now no condemnation for those who are in Christ Jesus"* (Rom 8:1); they are clothed in the righteousness of Christ and so their sin is covered. But unbelievers have no such covering for their sin, and must stand naked before the searching eyes of the holy God and hear those tragic words, *"I do not know you. Away from me, all you evildoers"* (Luke 13:27).

This is a difficult and unpopular doctrine, but as was stated earlier, we have no authority to make the teaching of the Scriptures more palatable; would that

---

* See the footnote on the previous page, page 125.

** But see my comment on Matt 25 regarding those who have never heard, Chapter 10, page 69.

we could! When we contemplate such teaching, our hearts, surely, are moved with deep sorrow at the fate of the lost. Paul experienced such sorrow when he considered the lost state of the majority of his fellow Jews. He says, *"I have great sorrow and unceasing anguish in my heart, (and) I could wish that I myself were ... cut off from Christ for the sake of my brothers, the people of Israel"* (Rom 9:2-4).

This is consistent with what God Himself feels, namely His own sorrow at the death of the wicked: *"As I live, says the Lord God, I have no pleasure in the death of the wicked, but that the wicked may turn from his way and live; turn back, turn back from your evil ways, for why will you die?"* (Ezek 33: 11) And did not Jesus weep over the fate of faithless Jerusalem? Yet there is a deeper law that operates, which we can scarcely begin to understand, that involves God's holiness and justice, and that ultimately He will be seen to have acted both righteously and justly in all that He does. Meanwhile, the doctrine of eternal punishment for the wicked and the unbelieving should spur us on to redouble our efforts to proclaim to all the gospel of God's offer of salvation in Christ – even if we have to do it with tears in our eyes.

After death: what? In human life, we are told, there are only two certainties, namely death and taxes! So it is probable that all of us will have to face death sooner or later – "probable" because Jesus <u>could</u> return before we die and overturn the expected course of events. But the question is bound to arise: "What happens after death?"

In respect of believers, the New Testament teaches us that death is *gain* because when we die we (our souls) go to be *with Christ* (2 Cor 5:8) to await the final resurrection and the re-uniting of our souls with our (resurrection) bodies. It is not in any way a punishment, but an open door into the presence of our Saviour, and something of which we therefore do not have to be afraid – we can, indeed, look forward to our own death with glad anticipation, knowing that we will be "with Jesus" immediately after death.

The Bible tell us that Jesus *"shared in our humanity so that by His death He might ... free those who all their lives were held in slavery by their fear of death"* (Heb 2: 14)? So the Revd David Watson, the well-known English evangelist, writer and pastor, speaking shortly before he died of liver cancer, was able to affirm, "The best is yet to be!". And this applies to all Christians – however satisfying and fulfilling our lives here on earth have been, the best is yet to be. We also have the wonderful assurance that not even death can separate us from God's love in Christ Jesus our Lord (Rom 8:38-39). This does not mean, of course, that we should not experience sorrow when Christian friends or family members die. It is only natural and human that we should do so, but our sorrow is mixed with joy that they are now "with the Lord".

As I see it, there is less clarity about the situation that unbelievers face when they die (as opposed to their final destiny, which is made abundantly clear in Scripture). The only text that possibly has a direct bearing on the matter is our Lord's parable of the rich man and Lazarus (Luke 16:19-21), and it is not at all clear to what extent the parable was meant to convey such detail. "A parable must not be pushed beyond its specific purpose" writes E.M. Blaiklock [109], and adds that the parable of the rich man and Lazarus "is designed to teach that the place and time of opportunity is here and now, and that the measure of earthly prosperity, social standing and wealth are no indication of a person's standing before God." It should not, therefore, be forced into giving details about the immediate destiny of the departed. So all that we can say about the unbelieving dead is that they go to *hades*, the place of departed spirits, to await the final judgement. Ultimately, both they and *hades* itself are to be cast into the lake of fire, which is the second death (Rev 20:14-15).

What is abundantly clear from the Scriptures is that there is no possibility of a "second chance" after death. The Bible never suggests that the final judgement depends on anything that we do after death, but only on what has happened in this life (Rom 2:5-10, 1 Cor 5:10, etc), since *"it is appointed for men to die once, and after that comes judgement"* (Heb 9:27). This also leads us to the conclusion that prayers for the dead are of no avail: those who have died "in Christ" are already with the Lord, and all their sins and failures have been dealt with through Christ's perfect atonement, their souls already rest in peace, and they have no need of our prayers, whereas those who are not "in Christ" when they die await God's final judgement -- their destiny is already sealed, settled by their sin and rebellion against God, or simply by their indifference, in this life. As sombre and unacceptable as these sentiments may be, the teaching of Scripture is clear enough, and I have no right to water it down in order to make it more user-friendly. So let us pray for, and work for the salvation of, people here and now, while we have an opportunity to do so and while they have an opportunity to respond, before it is too late. Remember that the night is coming when no further work will be done.

Heaven and Hell. We have noted that the final judgement results in a separation of humankind into two groups, namely those who are destined for heaven and those who are destined for hell. What do we mean by these terms?

By "hell" we mean a place or a state of eternal conscious separation from God, associated with sorrow and the torment of unavailing remorse ("if only ...."), and is the ultimate destiny of the wicked. Prepared as the place of punishment for the devil and his angels (Matt 25:41), it is also the destiny of all those whose names have not been written in the Book of Life (Rev 20:15). Some passages in the Bible suggest that there will be different degrees of sorrow for the wicked in hell (e.g. Luke 12: 47-48), just as there will be different degrees of reward for the saints in heaven (e.g. Luke 19:17,19; see below).

Heaven, on the other hand, is the place where God's presence is most completely manifested and where His people will spend eternity in His presence. Did not Jesus say (John 14:3), *"Do not let your hearts be troubled ... In my Father's house are many rooms ... I am going there to prepare a place for you "* (John 14:1-2). But we read also that there will be new heavens and a new earth, implying that the physical creation will be renewed (Rev 21:1; see also Rom 8:19-21) and we will continue to live in it and to care for it, now clothed in our "resurrection bodies" that will neither grow old nor become ill (1 Cor 15:35ff). At the same time *"God's dwelling will be with men, and He will live with them. They will be His people, and God Himself will be with them and be their God"* (Rev 21:3); notice that here we have both the final reiteration and also the fulfilment of the covenant promise. So the redeemed will inhabit the new heavens and the new earth and will forever be in God's presence, "lost in wonder, love and praise". And yes, there will be different degrees of rewards for God's people, and yet the joy of each one will be full and complete: there will be no room for envy or jealousy towards one another on account of differing "rewards" or "status"!

More than this I am unable to say. We may speculate about many other details of "heaven", but it will be no more than just that (i.e., speculation) because the reality will be far beyond our present ability to describe or to comprehend. I am quite content to leave it there, to live for God and to witness to the gospel as long as I am in this life, and then to enter His presence with praise and great humility. For as Paul says, quoting the prophet Isaiah, *"No eye has seen, no ear has heard, no mind has conceived, what God has prepared for those who love Him"* (1 Cor 2:9).

But what, you ask, about those who have never heard the gospel? I really cannot answer this question with any certainty. There is a hint – no more – in the early chapters of *Romans* that Gentiles who have never heard the gospel might be saved by their attitude towards the "light" that they have received from nature (Rom 2:12, 14-15; see also 1:20). The Bible tells us clearly that God will judge them on the basis of that light, but an equally possible interpretation of these passages is that the light they have received is sufficient to condemn them, leaving them *"without excuse"* and subject to God's wrath, rather than to exonerate them. Or is it perhaps possible that the parable of the sheep and the goats (Matt 25: 31-46) refers to those who have not heard about Jesus (*"all the nations"*, vs 31) as I suggested in Chapter 10, and who will be judged on their attitude towards those in need, since the word "nation" in Scripture often refers to the <u>gentile</u> nations who have had no share in the direct knowledge of God given through the Scriptures? But this is pure speculation. We <u>are</u> told that individuals within the Jewish nation have had the law, through which they can learn about God and come to know and to recognise their sinfulness; thus they are judged by the law, while gentiles, who have not had the law, will be judged according to other criteria, such as the light they have received, *"so that every mouth may be silenced and the whole world – Jew and Gentile – held accountable to God"* (Rom 2: 12 – 15; 3:19). All we can affirm is this, that when the time comes, God will be seen to have been both fair and just, and all His judgements will be declared to be righteous -- and with that we have to be content.

The hymn I have chosen with which to close this chapter speaks not only about the coming, and the coming-again, of Jesus, but also about our human ignorance in knowing and understanding the details of the ultimate will and plan of God. The hymn is printed on the next page.

1.   I cannot tell why He whom angels worship,
        Should set His love upon the sons of men;
    Or why, as Shepherd, He should seek the wanderers,
        To bring them back, they know not how or when.
    But this I know: that He was born of Mary,
        When Bethlehem's manger was His only home,
    And that he lived at Nazareth and laboured,
        And so the Saviour, Saviour of the world, is come.

2.   I cannot tell how silently He suffered,
        As with His peace He graced this place of tears,
    Or how His heart upon the cross was broken --
        The crown of pain to three and thirty years.
    But this I know: He heals the broken-hearted,
        And stays our sin, and calms our lurking fear,
    And lifts the burden from the heavy laden,
        For yet the Saviour, Saviour of the world, is here.

3.   I cannot tell how He will win the nations,
        How He will claim His earthly heritage;
    How satisfy the needs and aspirations
        Of East and West, of sinner and of sage.
    But this I know: all flesh shall see His glory,
        And He shall reap the harvest He has sown,
    And some glad day His sun will shine in splendour
        When He, the Saviour, Saviour of the world, is known.

4.   I cannot tell how all the lands shall worship,
        When at His bidding every storm is stilled.
    Or who can say how great the jubilation,
        When all the hearts of men with love are filled.
    But this I know: the skies will fill with rapture,
        And myriad, myriad human voices sing,
    And earth to heaven, and heaven to earth shall answer:
        At last the Saviour, Saviour of the world is King!

William Young Fullerton

Chapter 17 : THE BIBLE AND THE WORD OF GOD

Any reader who has persevered this far will have realised that I have attempted to base my faith, my understanding of Christian doctrine and, hence, what I have written, on the teaching of the Bible, albeit "as I see it"! And where I appear to have departed from the doctrinal position of my own, or any other, Christian denomination, I have done so only because I have wished my teaching to be faithful to my understanding of the Biblical testimony, rather than simply to reflect a particular denominational confession of faith. Evangelical Christians the world over share a love for the Bible and its teaching, and hold it in high regard as the authoritative record of God's revelation of Himself to humankind. We know that God's ultimate revelation came through the Word of God, who is our Lord Jesus Christ, but even so it is still the Bible's testimony that tells us all we know about His coming, His life, and the significance of His death and resurrection.

The word (Word) of God. For the Christian, the term "word of God" can have different meanings, namely, Jesus Christ, the eternal Son of God (the **W**ord of God, John 1:1-2,14) and the Bible (the **w**ord of God); note the attempt I have made to differentiate between the two usages of "word". There is a further usage that needs to be considered, and rejected. It is common practice in certain theological circles to aver that the Bible *becomes* the word of God only when the Holy Spirit speaks to our spirits through its message; at other times it remains simply a record of mankind's search for God. Two comments need to be made in this connection. Firstly, this view leads to a highly subjective view of Scripture, and denudes it of any real authority to regulate our beliefs and actions. In the second place, the Bible is not primarily an account of man's search for God, but of God's search for humankind in order to bring it back into fellowship with its Creator. The historic Christian understanding of the Scriptures has been that they proclaim objective truths that are true in and of themselves, whatever impact they might make on a particular reader, and no matter what his or her response might be. This is not to deny that it is the Holy Spirit who opens our eyes to the wonders of God's grace revealed in the Scriptures, and helps us to apply its teaching to our lives.

One further view, closely related to what has just been said, is that the Bible "contains the word of God" – in other words, that some of the Bible is the word of God and that other parts are not. But how are we to decide? By labelling those sections that appeal to us as being the word of God, and those that do not as not being the word of God? Clearly, this, too, is a highly subjective stance to take, and once again undermines Biblical authority. Yes, the Bible does contain the word of God, but only in the sense that a bucket filled to the brim contains water!

We note that on numerous occasions the writers of the Bible use phrases such as "The word of the Lord came to …", "This is what the Lord says …." "The Lord spoke all these words …" "The Lord said, 'Write down these words …' ", etc, thus emphasising that the Bible is, above all, God's word to us, and we are urged to pay close attention to what it says (e.g. Luke 8:18; Heb 2:1; 2 Pet 1:19).

Inspiration. It is an unfortunate accident of history that early translators of the Bible into English used the word "inspiration" in their translation of 2 Tim 3:16, and in so doing introduced a word into the theological vocabulary that is still in current usage today. So the Authorised Version renders 2 Tim 3:16 as follows:

> *"All scripture is given by inspiration of God, and is profitable for doctrine, for reproof, for correction, for instruction in righteousness…"*

The Greek word used in this passage and translated "inspiration" does emphatically not mean "inspired by God". What it says of Scripture is not that it is "breathed into by God", nor that it is the product of God's "inbreathing" into (i.e., *inspiration of*) its human authors, but "that it is breathed out by God, or 'God-breathed'; thus it is the product of the creative breath of God" [110]. Since the "breath of God" is in Scripture the symbol of God's almighty creative power (Ps 33:6, etc), Paul is saying that Scripture has been brought into being by the creative power of God, and that it is His authoritative word to us.

A similar idea is conveyed in 2 Pet 1:21, *"For prophecy never had its origin in the will of man, but men spoke from God as they were moved by the Holy Spirit."* We have here a clear denial that (true) prophecy owes its origin to human initiative, and the equally clear assertion that its source lies in God: it was indeed spoken by men, but the men who spoke it "spoke from God as they were moved (literally 'carried along') by the Holy Spirit." And in his second epistle (2 Pet 3:16), Peter places Paul's writings on the same level of authority as the 'God-breathed' writings of the Old Testament. We note, then, that the Biblical writers do not think of the Scriptures as a human product breathed into ("inspired") by the Holy Spirit in order to add an "extra influence" to what has been written, but as a divine product brought about through the instrumentality of men as they were controlled and moved by God's purpose and carried along by the power of the Holy Spirit in order to accomplish His will. As the NIV Study Bible expresses it [111], "In the production of Scripture both God and man were active participants. God was the source of the content of Scripture, so that what it says is what God has said. But the human author also actively spoke; he was more than simply a recorder. Yet what he said came from God."

One further point needs to be clarified under the sub-heading *Inspiration*. Although we say that the Bible is the inspired word of God, it does not mean that all the actions recorded in the Bible were inspired by God or met with His approval. The worship of the golden calf (Ex 32:4) and all the other instances and examples of idolatry among the Israelites, the covetousness of king Ahab which led to the murder of Naboth (1 Kings 21), and the adultery and murder committed by king David in the shameful episode involving Bathsheba (2 Sam 11), were not inspired actions – Biblical inspiration merely safeguarded the accuracy of the recording of these events. Similarly, the rash promise made by Jephthah (Judges 11) was not an inspired act, even though it is recorded in the inspired writings, possibly as a warning to all of an example <u>not</u> to be followed!

The human element. Lest the impression be given that I envisage a "mechanical" process of inspiration in which God dictated His message to the various writers who acted simply as scribes or "shorthand typists", it must be stated emphatically that this is not the case. In revealing His word and His will, God in no way overrode the personalities, backgrounds (including cultural backgrounds), interests and literary styles of the Biblical prophets and writers. Rather, in His providence, God prepared individuals with their own unique personalities who would use their freedom of expression to write the words that He desired, using the literary styles and genre with which they felt comfortable. Thus "if God wished to give His people a series of letters like those of Paul, He prepared a Paul to write them, and the Paul He brought to the task was a Paul who spontaneously would write just such letters" [112]. So the Bible contains a large number of types of literature that reflect the personalities and experiences of the individual writers, as well as their own particular style of writing and their cultural background, and it is important that the text be interpreted with due regard to all these factors, and especially with regard to the literary genre (including symbolism) employed *. The human element in Scripture is an important aspect of the way in which God has carried out His purposes, and we rejoice that it should be so.

Does this human element not, by its very nature, mean that the final product -- the Bible – must be severely flawed? Here we may turn to a Biblical analogy to illustrate the human element in Scripture: the person of the Lord Jesus Christ Himself. We saw in chapter five that He had two natures, a divine nature as God, and a human nature as truly man. And just as in the person of our Lord, so both human and divine qualities can be recognised in Scripture. But we can take this further; just as Jesus Christ, though truly man, was God's authentic revelation of Himself, so Scripture, though a truly human product, is also the authentic revelation from God. Of course, if the New Testament is simply the religious self-expression of the early Church, then it will be subject to the limitations inevitable for any finite mind trying to contain infinity. And it would be no more authoritative than the religious experiences of people living in any other period during the history of the Church – and, indeed, no more authoritative than the experiences of any other religious group, whether Christian or not. But if, as Christians down through the centuries have maintained, the Bible is primarily and essentially God's word concerning Himself, then it is not an imperfect attempt by men to express their experiences of God, but God's infallible declaration which is objectively true, even though it bears the stamp of the writers' personalities and culture (Heb 1:1-3) **.

There are a number of problems that confront us when we assert that Scripture is God's infallible declaration, many of which cannot be solved given our present state of knowledge. But our understanding of the contexts and aims of the writers is continually expanding, our knowledge of their use of language (especially their use of idiom and nuance) is increasing, and through textual criticism we are approaching ever more closely to the original text. At the same time, archaeology is uncovering more and more of the culture of ancient

---

* It is not my purpose to comment in detail on ways of interpreting Scripture. The interested reader is referred to the excellent work by Alan M Stibbs, "*Understanding God's Word*", The Inter-Varsity Fellowship, London, 1950, and the much more recent work, *Abusing Scripture*, by Manfred T Brauch, Inter-Varsity Press, Downers Grove, IL, 2009.

** For a fuller treatment of this matter, see references **113** and **114**.

times -- the social and religious contexts in which much of the Bible was written. We can thus expect many of our current difficulties to disappear with further advances in our understanding, just as has happened frequently in the past. A number of other problems are capable of solution if we bear in mind that symbolism is a legitimate literary vehicle: there is nothing inconsistent in recognising that real events, such as creation, Adam and Eve, and the fall of humankind, may be recorded in a highly symbolic manner. A further point often missed by critics is the importance of the *phenomenological* approach of Hebrew culture – phenomena were normally described as they appeared, and not in terms of underlying scientific theories or philosophical speculation. "When the sun stood still" (Josh 10:13) does not compel us to believe that the earth temporarily stopped rotating about its axis (what disastrous consequences that would have had!); it is no less accurate than our use of "sunrise" and "sunset"! An unusual occurrence of refraction in the atmosphere could have caused the observed phenomenon – and such have been recorded in the past [115]. However, there are other ways of interpreting this passage, and hence other possible explanations for what occurred.

The teaching and example of Jesus. In this, the final section of the book, I wish to refer very briefly to the attitude of our Lord Jesus Christ to the Scriptures. We remember how He was tempted by the devil (Matt 4:1-10) and how He blunted the devil's attacks with quotations from the Old Testament. He described the Old Testament law as "the word of God" (Mark 7:13) and explained that the whole Old Testament contained references to Himself as the Christ (Luke 24:25) and that it enshrined the Father's testimony about the Son (John 5:37-40). He claimed that He had came to fulfil the "Law and the Prophets", i.e. the whole of the Old Testament, thus clearly upholding the authority of the Old Testament, and He accused His detractors of not believing what God had said through the writings of Moses (John 5:45-47). Wenham summarises it as follows [114], "The evidence is clear: to Christ the Old Testament was true, authoritative, inspired. To Him the God of the Old Testament was the living God, the teaching of the Old Testament was the teaching of the living God. To Him, what Scripture said, God said". Then, speaking of His own words, Jesus proclaimed that they would *"never pass away"* (Matt 24:35), and it was He who promised to send the Holy Spirit both to lead the apostles into truth and to bring to their remembrance all that He had said to them and taught them (John 14:26). So Packer [116] writes, "We conclude, then, that we must reckon seriously with the fact that Christ accepted the principle of Biblical authority … and embodied it unchanged in Christianity".

As believers, the Bible is our ultimate authority, whether as to how we should live or what we should believe, and also as to our understanding of the will and purposes of God. It has been my authority as I have sought to live for God's glory as a Christian, it has been my authority in my preaching, and it has been my authority as I have written this book. In places I will have misinterpreted its testimony. At times I have failed to live up to its teachings, and I have not always followed the example that Jesus has set me. But this same Bible assures me that, through His atoning love, my failures and my shortcomings are covered by His righteousness: they are forgiven and forgotten. And I am challenged again by the words in Luke 11:28: "Blessed are those who hear the word of God and obey it".

1. Lord, Thy word abideth,
    And our footsteps guideth;
   Who its truth believeth
    Light and joy receiveth.

2. Who can tell the pleasure,
    Who recount the treasure,
   By Thy word imparted
    To the humble hearted?

3. When the storms are o'er us,
    And dark clouds before us,
   Then thy light directeth,
    And our way protecteth.

4. When our foes are near us,
    Then Thy word doth cheer us;
   Word of consolation,
    Message of salvation.

5. Word of mercy giving,
    Succour to the living;
   Word of life supplying
    Comfort to the dying.

6. O that we discerning
    Its most holy learning,
   Lord, may love and fear Thee,
    Evermore be near Thee.

Henry Williams Baker **(1821 – 1877)**

Literature References

1. (a) Macarthur, John. *The Battle for the Beginning*, Nelson Books, 2001, page 24. (b) Roos, JTH, *He Made the Stars Also*, to be published.
2. *New Bible Dictionary*, Inter-Varsity Fellowship, London 1962 pp 529 ff (article *Holiness*).
3. Grudem W, *Systematic Theology*, Inter-Varsity Press, Leicester 1994, p 267.
4. Grudem W, *op cit*, p 267.
5. Grudem W, *op cit*, p187.
6. Hammond TC, *In Understanding be Men*, Inter-Varsity Fellowship, London 1954, p 74.
7. Grudem W, *op cit*, pp 442 – 443.
8. New Bible Dictionary, p 556 (article *Image*).
9. Grudem W, *op cit*, p 159.
10. Berkhof L, *Systematic Theology*, The Banner of Truth Trust, London, 1969, p 60.
11. Hammond TC, op cit, p 45.
12. Grudem W, *op cit*, p 173
13. Keller W, *The Bible as History*, Hodder & Stoughton, London 1956, pp 95 – 96.
14. Kidner D, Tyndale Commentary *Genesis*, The Tyndale Press, London 1967, p 135.
15. Collins, FS, *The Language of God*, Free Press, New York, 2006, page 45.
16. Thomas, WH Griffith, *The Principles of Theology*, Church Book Room Press, London 1956 (1930), p 252 (footnote 1, quoting Liddon, *Some elements of religion*, p 191).
17. Kitchen KA, *Ancient Orient and Old Testament*, The Tyndale Press, London 1966.
18. WJ Beasley, *Creations Amazing Architect*, Gospel Literature Service, Bombay, 1970 page 113.
19. Schroeder, *Genesis and the Big Bang*. Bantam Books, New York, 1992, pages 97 – 98.

20. Denton, Michael. *Evolution: A theory in Crisis.* Adler and Adler, Bethesda, Md., 1986.

21. Johnson, Philip E, *Darwin on Trial.* InterVarsity Press, Downers Grove, Ill., 1991.

22. Pearce EK Victor, *Who was Adam?* Paternoster Press, London, 1969, page 80.

23. Craig, The Revd GS, private communication to the author.

24. *The Smithsonian,* May 1987, pages 127 – 135.

25. Warfield BB, *Biblical Foundations,* The Tyndale Press, London, 1958, p 80

26. Lewis CS, *Mere Christianity,* Geoffrey Bles, London 1952, p 119 (Title of Book IV)

27. Warfield BB, *op cit,* p 105.

28. NIV study Bible, Comment on Col 2:9.

29. Warfield BB, *op cit,* p 91.

30. Grudem Wayne, *op cit,* p 227.

31. NIV Study Bible, comment on Gen 1:2.

32. Grudem Wayne, *op cit,* p 249.

33. Grudem Wayne, *op cit,* p 231.

34. JB Phillips, *Your God is too Small.* Epworth Press, London 1952.

35. Warfield BB, *op cit,* pp 97 – 98.

36. Morris, L. *Revelation,* Tyndale New Testament Commentaries, The Tyndale Press, London 1969, p 82.

37. Amplified New Testament, Zondervan Publishing House, Grand Rapids 1965.

38. Grudem Wayne, *op cit,* pp 243 – 244

39. Warfield BB, *op cit,* p 148.

40. NIV Study Bible, comment on John 1:18.

41. Life Application Study Bible based on the New Living Translation text, Tyndale House Publishers, Wheaton, Illinois 1996. Comment on John 1:18

42. Torrey, RA, *What the Bible Teaches,* Fleming H Revell Co., New York 1933, p 95.

43. Carson, HM, *Dawn or twilight?*. IVP, Leicester, 1976, pp 22 – 23.
44. Morris, Leon, *The Lord from Heaven*. Inter-Varsity Fellowship, London 1958, pp 49 - 52
45. Grudem Wayne, *op cit*, p 539.
46. White RS, quoted by Morris, reference [**44**], pp 50 – 51.
47. Grudem Wayne, *op cit*, p 541.
48. Morris, Leon, *The Person of Christ*, The Christian Faith Series, Church Book Room Press Ltd, London 1960, p 15.
49. Kitwood TM, *What is Human*. Inter-Varsity Press, Leicester 1970, p. 94.
50. Kitwood TM, *op cit*, p 97.
51. Hammond, TC, *op cit*, p 71.
52. Grudem, Wayne, *op cit*, p 481.
53. Quoted by Clyde Kilby in *A Mind Awake*, Geoffrey Bles, London 1968, pp 22-24.
54. **(a)** Lewis CS, *Mere Christianity*, Geoffrey Bles, London 1952, Book 3, chapter 10; **(b)** Lewis CS, *Transposition and Other Addresses*, Geoffrey Bles, London, chapter 2; **(c)** Lewis CS, *The Four Loves*, Geoffrey Bles, London 1960, chapter 1.
55. Kitwood, *op cit*, p 96.
56. *Miracles*, Geoffrey Bles, London 1947, chapter 14.
57. Lewis CS, *Mere Christianity*, Book 2, chapter 3.
58. Roos, *op cit*, chapter 7.
59. Lewis CS, *Prince Caspian*, Geoffrey Bles, London 1951, chapter 15.
60. Phillips, JB, *Your God is too Small*, Epworth Press, London 1952, p 93f.
61. NIV Study Bible, comment on John 10:18.
62. Encyclopaedia Britannica, 1987; Eerdmans Bible Dictionary, Eerdmans, 1987, Article *Crucifixion*.
63. Torrey RA, *op cit*, page 225.
64. NIV Study Bible, comment on Ephesians 5:18.
65. Morris Leon, *Spirit of the Living God*, Inter-Varsity Fellowship, London, 1960, p 94.

66. Foulkes Francis, *The Epistle of Paul to the Ephesians*, Tyndale New Testament Commentaries, The Tyndale Press, London, 1963, p 136.

67. Morris Leon, *Op cit*, p 101.

68. Stibbs, AM and Packer, JI, *The Spirit within you*, Hodder and Stoughton, London, 1967, p 60.

69. Grudem Wayne, *Op cit*, pp 857-858.

70. NIV Study Bible, comment on 1 Peter 2:5.

71. Grudem Wayne, *Op cit*, pp 867-868.

72. Deborah Ford, *Mission in the 21st Century*, in *Wider World*, Magazine of the Presbyterian Church in Ireland, Sept. 2004, p 18.

73. Cunningham William, *Historical Theology*, Banner of Truth, London 1969, Volume I, pages 82, 84. (First published in 1862.)

74. Hewitt Thomas, *Tyndale New Testament Commentary on Hebrews*, Tyndale Press, London 1960; NIV Study Bible, comment on Hebrews 12: 1.

75. Torrey, RA, *op cit*, p 478.

76. NIV Study Bible, comment on Gen 11:31.

77. Grudem Wayne, *op cit*, p 522.

78. Grudem Wayne, *op cit*, p 978.

79. Motyer, JA, New Bible Dictionary. Article: *Baptism*.

80. Cunningham, *The Reformers and the Theology of the Reformation*, The Banner of Truth Trust, London 1967 (1862), page 250 (see pp 240 –253).

81. Watson Peter, Series of articles in *Presbyterian Life*, April 1989 (?).

82. Grudem Wayne, *op cit*, p 954.

83. Macleod Donald, *Presbyterian Worship*, John Knox Press, Atlanta 1981, pp 49, 51.

84. Bromily GW, *The Baptism of Infants*, The Church Book Room Press, London 1955, p 1; Edersheim, A, *The Life and Times of Jesus the Messiah*, Vol II, Pickering and Inglis, London 1959, Appendix XII (page 746).

85. *Jews for Jesus Newsletter*. January 1991, page 6.

86. Martin RP in New Bible Dictionary, p. 750. Article: *The Lord's Supper*.

87. The *Consensus of Tigurinus*, XXI (a confession drawn up by the reformers and agreed to by both Calvin and Zwingle as expressing their common faith).

88. Grudem Wayne, *op cit*, p 995.

89. Edersheim, A. The Life and Times of Jesus the Messiah (volume II), Pickering & Inglis, London,1959 (1883), pp 34 – 35.

90. Tasker RVG, *The Gospel according to St John*, Tyndale New Testament Commentaries, The Tyndale Press, London 1960, p 96.

91. Ryle JC, *Expository Thoughts on the Gospels*, James Clarke & Co Ltd, London 1957 (1856), p 396.

92. Bruce R, *The Mystery of the Lord's Supper*, James Clarke & Co Ltd, London 1958, pp 90, 98.

93. From Willet's Synopsis Papismi, quoted by William Cunningham, *The Reformers and the Theology of the Reformation*, The Banner of Truth Trust, London, 1967 (1862), p 227, slightly paraphrased for the sake of clarity.

94. Kuyper RB, *The Glorious Body of Christ*, Banner of Truth Trust, London 1966, p 210

95. Holland JAB, Private communication to the author.

96. Carson HM, *Dawn or Twilight?*, The Inter-Varsity Press, Leicester 1976, p 109.

97. Kevan Ernest F, *The Lord's Supper*, Evangelical Press, London 1966, p 16.

98. Ryle JC, *Practical Religion*, James Clarke and Co. Ltd., London 1959 (1898?), page 115. See also his book *Knots Untied*, from the same publisher.

99. Anonymous, *A Declaration of the Truth revealed in the Bible*, published by the Christadelphians (Logos Publications, South Australia), 1982, p 29.

100. (a) Reference 99, page 32. (b) Davidson, Bill, *The Devil and Demons: A New Approach*, 3rd edition, page 19 (no publisher or date given).

101. Peterson, Robert & Martha, *Like a Roaring Lion*, OMF Books, Singapore, 1989.

102. Motyer JA, *The Tests of Faith*, Inter-Varsity Press, London 1970, pp 88 - 89.

103. Foulkes Francis, *The Epistle of Paul to the Ephesians*, Tyndale New Testament Commentaries, The Tyndale Press, London, 1963, p 175.

104. Grudem Wayne, *op cit.*
105. Grudem Wayne, *op cit*, p1104.
106. Ladd GE, *A Commentary on the Revelation of John*, Eerdmans, Grand Rapids, Michigan 1972, p 22.
107. NIV Study Bible, Note on 1 Thes 5:3.
108. Morris Leon, *The Cross in the New Testament*, The Paternoster Press, Exeter 1967, p 362.
109. Blaiklock EM., *The Daily Commentary, Vol 3*, Scripture Union, London 1974, pp 228 – 229 (comments on Luke 16).
110. Warfield BB, *op cit*, p 47.
111. NIV Study Bible, comment on 2 Pet 1:21.
112. Warfield BB, *op cit*, page 67.
113. Packer JI, *'Fundamentalism' and the Word of God*, The Intervarsity Fellowship, London, 1958, pp 83 – 84; Warfield, B.B., *op cit*, pp 74 - 75.
114. Wenham JW, *Christ and the Bible*, The Tyndale Press, London 1972, p 37.
115. Short A Rendle, *Modern Discovery and the Bible*, 2nd Edition, Inter-Varsity Fellowship, London 1949, pp 155 – 156.
116. Packer JI, *op cit*, p 62.

www.ingramcontent.com/pod-product-compliance
Lightning Source LLC
Chambersburg PA
CBHW061658040426
42446CB00010B/1804